SOUTH END SYNDICATE

SOUTH END SYNDICATE

HOW I TOOK OVER THE GENOVESE SPRINGFIELD CREW

ANTHONY ARILLOTTA

With Joe Bradley

HAMILCAR
PUBLICATIONS
BOSTON

ISBN: 978-1-949590-76-0

hamilcarpubs.com

Aut viam inveniam aut faciam

For my father
—Anthony

For Lynne and Chris
—Joe

CONTENTS

*Look back over the past, with its changing empires,
that rose and fell, and you can foresee the future too.*
—**Marcus Aurelius**

FOREWORD

Growing up as a child in Springfield, I didn't know the name of our mayor or the chief of police. But I knew the name "Big Nose Sam" Cufari. He was a captain in the Genovese crime family and the Mafia boss in our city for decades, and he was respected and feared by many in the community.

▼ ▼ ▼

I passed the Springfield police exam and was selected to attend the police academy in June 1986. After working on patrol on the dogwatch for three years, I moved to the second shift, and soon after I was assigned to work in the gang unit.

There were around six hundred cops in the department at the time and the city was split into eighteen districts. Working in the gang car allowed us to patrol the entire city and not just one district like other officers—we were proactive law enforcement.

My partner and I were downtown when a call came in for the theft of a mink coat at a restaurant, Cara Mia, in the South End. We were familiar with that restaurant because it was owned by Al Bruno, the Mafia boss of Springfield. After arriving at the scene, we spoke with the hostess. She told us a woman's coat was stolen from the rack at the top of the stairs, so we put it out over the radio and began looking around the area.

A couple blocks away, we spotted a guy walking down the street carrying a mink coat. We grabbed him and the coat and put him in the back seat.

"Where did you get the coat?" I asked.

"I bought it for my mom," he said.

"Yeah, where did you buy it?" my partner asked.

"From some bitch on the corner."

"How much did you pay?" he asked.

"Twenty-five."

We could tell this was an expensive coat, probably worth over a grand.

"You're a liar," I said. "You stole this from Cara Mia restaurant. Do you know who owns that restaurant?"

"No."

"Al Bruno, the Italian Mafia boss of Springfield," I said. "They call him 'Al the Butcher.' Do you know why?"

"No, I don't."

"Because he is known for cutting off the hands of people who steal from him," I said. "We're taking you back there to see him now."

I made up the butcher story on the fly to scare him—it worked.

"No, you can't do that," he stammered. "You're the police; you have to arrest me."

He was getting nervous and jittery. "Nope, we're taking you to the restaurant."

"Arrest me," he said. "I did it; I confess. You have to take me to the police station!"

I looked at my partner and he smirked and nodded, and I knew we were thinking the same thing.

We went back to the restaurant, and I went inside and was met by Bruno. I told him what happened and that we told the thief that his nickname was "The Butcher."

Bruno smiled. "Bring him and the coat up here," he said.

We took him up the stairs and Bruno was waiting. My partner handed him the coat and we introduced the thief to Al.

"Take him to the kitchen," Bruno said.

As we brought him into the kitchen, we thought he was going to piss himself.

"You have to arrest me," he pleaded.

Al came in a picked up a meat cleaver. "This is the guy who stole from me?" he said. "I should chop off your hand."

He was struggling to get away and crying out. "Please don't do me like this. You can arrest me. I'm sorry!"

Bruno slammed the cleaver down onto the counter. "If you ever come here or steal from me again, I'll cut off your fucking hand," Bruno said with dark eyes.

"I won't, I promise," the thief cried.

I moved into the other room to have a word with Bruno. "Do you want us to arrest him?"

"No. Just have a hard talk with him," he said. "You and your partner can come here every Sunday for dinner on me."

We had orchestrated what Bruno was going to do before we brought him in the kitchen. Bruno said he just wanted to scare the shit out of him, and it worked.

We didn't loosen him up like Bruno asked. We figured he got the message—no need to slap him around.

The following Sunday we went to Cara Mia for dinner, and we ordered anything we wanted on the menu. This continued every Sunday for months and we ate like kings for free—we always left a big tip.

▼ ▼ ▼

When I was asked by a mutual friend to speak with a guy who wanted advice on writing a book, I agreed. She didn't say who he was, just that she had known him for years and he wanted to tell his story.

On a three-way call, I learned who he was when she introduced him as Anthony Arillotta. I never knew him personally, even though he had lived at his grandmother's across the street from my parents' house. I also knew he was a former Mob boss of Springfield and that he had gone to prison for murder.

He asked me if I'd be interested in writing his story, and I told him it wasn't my genre. At that time, I had written five novels and a screenplay. All of them were fiction crime thrillers, and this was a true-crime story. After talking for a while, I agreed to meet him for lunch.

We met in Glastonbury, and I found him to be an interesting gentleman. He was polite, well dressed, and he didn't curse like I expected he would. We had a nice conversation over lunch—I liked him.

I told him I would think about it, and after meeting a couple more times for dinner and drinks, I agreed to take on the project.

▼ ▼ ▼

Looking back to when I was a cop, I now realize that I made some bad errors in judgment. When we are in the thick of things, we don't always see the big picture and think so clearly. I have my regrets, but found consolation by admitting my mistakes, making reparations, and evolving. Today, I'm a much different person than I was back then—I have found my peace in knowing this.

As I've become professionally and personally involved with Anthony, I believe he has some regrets of his own, and he too is a different person today. Over the past few years, we have spent a lot of time together and I now consider him a friend.

Joe Bradley
June 2024

KILLING
GARY

PROLOGUE

The first time I met Gary Westerman was in 1995 at Antonio's Grinders in the South End. I noticed Freddy Geas with another guy who was a fairly good-sized decent looking character. He wore a brown leather coat and dress pants.

"Freddy, what's going on?" I gave him a quick hug.

"Nothin', just getting a bite. Bingy, this is Gary."

"How ya doing?" I shook his hand.

"Good to meet you," he said. "You're a legend in the prison system. I figured you to be around six-foot-five and two-hundred-and-fifty pounds. The stories on the inside made me think you were a much bigger guy."

"Well as you can see, I'm not. But don't let my size fool you."

I was flattered that I had such a reputation in the system, and I took a liking to Westerman. Ty Geas had connected with Westerman while doing time, and he eventually introduced him to Freddy.

Westerman had moved to the Springfield area in his late teens. He was first arrested when he was nineteen years old for robbing stores at the Eastfield

Mall in Springfield. He and two other guys gained access to the roof and slithered through air conditioning vents to get into the mall. They had stolen more than twenty-eight thousand dollars in jewelry, furs, leather coats, and pharmaceuticals. He was sentenced to prison in 1973 for robbery, and this would be the first of many trips to state penitentiaries throughout his life.

In 1986, Westerman was arrested for transporting cocaine from Florida to Springfield. He was arrested along with Frankie Campiti, a suspect in several gangland murders, and he was sentenced to do his time in Norfolk Prison in Dedham, Massachusetts.

When he got out in the early Nineties, he hooked up with Freddy, and they began robbing drug dealers, committing robberies, and selling large quantities of narcotics. Their crime spree ended when they were arrested in 1996 for stealing a trailer truck filled with computers. Freddy was concerned that Westerman was going to talk to get a reduced sentence and told me he wanted to kill him. "Two can keep a secret if one is dead," he said.

A week later, our associate Louie Santos went to Westerman's apartment to ask him to come along for a robbery while we waited in a van with a gun. His girlfriend answered the door and said he had gone out and she didn't know where he went, so Louie left.

Freddy, Louie, and I had planned on picking him up to ask him if he wanted to help us rob a drug dealer. We figured he would jump at the chance for a quick score, and we knew he liked the thrill of the action. Once we got him into the van, Freddy would shoot him in the head, and we would dump his body.

Anyway, that was our plan; but at that point, we knew we couldn't whack Westerman after his girlfriend saw Louie's face. We had no way of knowing she would be at his place when Louie went to the door. If he ended up murdered, his girlfriend could identify Louie in a photo array and line-up.

Less than a year later, Freddy was sentenced to three years in prison, and Westerman got four. The hit didn't happen at that point.

My wife's younger sister Sandra was a wild nineteen-year-old who enjoyed doing drugs and having sex with many partners. She was into ecstasy, cocaine, and penis. While I was separated from Irene, I banged her several times.

After Westerman got out of prison in 2002, he ended up going steady with her, and her parents weren't happy about it. Freddy had gotten out a year earlier, and he and Westerman were back together, committing crimes on the street. It was all about making money. Westerman was one of those guys who was always up to making moves on the street and he was pretty good at pulling off capers.

Freddy didn't like or trust Westerman—none of us did. He was a snake in the grass, and we knew eventually we would have to cut his head off.

My in-laws owned Zonin's deli on Main Street, and it was a popular place to get Italian sausage, meat, and cheese. I stopped in to grab some food, and my father-in-law started on me. He was complaining that my sister-in-law was only nineteen years old, and she was seeing Westerman, who was forty-nine. He said Westerman had her doing drugs and that they were disrespectful to him and his wife, and he wanted me to talk to Westerman and get him to stop seeing her. This went on for weeks. Every time I saw him, he was riding me about Westerman. Finally, I approached Westerman and asked him to find another girl. I told him my in-laws were driving me crazy, and they didn't want him dating their daughter. The next time I saw my father-in-law, he began harassing me again.

"I thought you were a big shot and had street cred. This guy doesn't listen to you or fear you. He still refuses to break off the relationship. He's disrespecting you, me, and my wife."

"He's still seeing her?" I said in a hollering whisper.

"Yes, he was just here to pick her up yesterday and she never made it back home last night," he said as if he'd just sunk his teeth into a rotten egg.

Gary
Westerman

An intense heated feeling hit the back of my neck. I made it clear to him he was to stop seeing her, and he completely defied my command. At that point, I was getting pumped up and at the end of my rope with Westerman. I had to kill him.

"Alright, I'll take care of it."

▼ ▼ ▼

I went to Dicky Jovelet's house to get the guns—he was holding my arsenal of weapons. Then I called my friend Michael DeCaro and asked him to give me a ride to have a hard talk with Westerman.

The plan was in motion. Freddy was going to go out to dinner with Westerman at the Federal Hill Club in Agawam. Ten minutes before they were going to leave, Freddy would beep me, and we would be waiting outside in a car with guns and wearing masks. After they exited the restaurant, DeCaro would pull the car up, and I would jump out and shoot Westerman—leaving him to die in the street. It was a simple plan. We had put a stolen plate on the car in case someone saw us leaving the scene.

My beeper sounded, and I told DeCaro to pull up to the side of the building because they would have to walk right past us to get to the parking lot. We masked up, and I told DeCaro to drive up to them real slow as they walked out, and I'd jump out and start shooting at point-blank range. DeCaro began to pull up as they came out, but they turned in the other direction, away from us. Westerman had a Porsche and he had parked it in a spot by the street, not in the back parking lot where we thought he would be parked. I told DeCaro to hurry up and drive up to them so that I could get him, but it was too late. They both got into the car, and I knew it was too dangerous for Freddy while he sat next to him in such a small car. We had to abort the hit. Westerman had no clue how close he came to meeting his maker that night.

As time went on, Westerman began to earn favor with my in-laws. He was taking my mother-in-law out to fancy dinners and buying her gifts, so I backed off because they were getting along. And my father-in-law wasn't busting my balls anymore.

A few months later, my sister-in-law, who agreed to be the Godmother of my daughter, blew off the Christening and ran off and got married to Westerman. I was really pissed off because she left us at the altar without a Godmother. Soon after, I found out that Westerman was an informant for the State Police. This was the straw that broke the camel's back.

My office was in West Springfield at my cigar shop, and I asked Freddy and Ty to meet me there. Inside, I told them I was going to kill Westerman, and I asked for their help, and they agreed.

On November 4, 2003, I drove to an East Longmeadow restaurant where Emilio Fusco was eating lunch with a girl. I told him about the hit and asked if he wanted to come along. He said yes. We left the restaurant and had Tony Vitrano drive us to my stash house in Agawam, where I hid my drugs and kept some guns.

Freddy had told Westerman that he and Ty were going to hit a drug house and rob them of cash and weed. He asked Westerman if he wanted to come along, and he agreed.

Tony dropped me and Fusco up the street from my stash house, and we walked over and waited in the garage for Freddy, Ty, and Westerman to show up.

It was around 7:30 p.m. when we heard the truck pulling down the driveway. As they entered the house, we stood in the garage with two shovels that we would use to fill in the hole after dumping Westerman into it. We could hear the three of them walking around the house, and we listened as the footsteps got louder and were moving faster. We could hear Westerman making grunting sounds as Ty shot him with a .22 caliber handgun, but we could barely hear the shots because he had a silencer on the gun. Ty emptied an entire clip into Westerman until he ran out of bullets.

We ran into the house to find Freddy and Ty wrestling with Westerman, who was trying to get away. Even though he was shot several times, Westerman was a big guy, and he was fighting for his life. They were having a hard time controlling him. Blood was spattered all over the walls and on the floor. The three of them were also covered in blood. It looked like a scene in a slasher film. At that point, I knew we had to stop Westerman, and I hit him over the head with my shovel, and Fusco did the same. We began whacking him in the face and head with our shovels until he was out cold. We literally beat his brains in. Now, we had to get him to the gravesite, so we started to drag his body across the yard, and he was heavy. A minute later, he woke up, so we beat him over the head again—much worse than the first time.

Finally, we dragged him to the hole and pushed him in. I was concerned that he might not be dead, and I didn't want to bury him alive, so I told Freddy to shoot him in the head to make sure. After a brief hesitation, Freddy took out a .38 caliber revolver and he shot him. We filled in the hole and left Westerman in the resting place he would occupy for the next seven years.

GETTING
MY BUTTON

CHAPTER 1

t was on this day that my life would change forever. The existence I had
known would never be the same. It was August 11, 2003, and as I drove to
the Bronx in New York City that morning, it was wet outside. It had rained
for twelve days straight, and I was tired of it. At the time, it had broken a
record for consecutive days of rain, and it came with relentless humidity.

I arrived at Nebraska Steak House just before 11:00 a.m., and I was the
first one there. Three other guys who were summoned would arrive shortly
after. I walked into the restaurant, which was closed to the public. A guy I
knew as Joe, a captain with the family, came over, pointed to a table, and
told me to take a seat, before walking away. My palms were growing moist,
and my mouth was as dry as sandpaper. My mind drifted to the scene in
Goodfellas where Joe Pesci walked into a room to become a Made guy and
was shot in the back of the head, which was haunting me as I waited.

A few minutes later, Joe returned, placed a large cigar ashtray down, and
told me to put all my jewelry and cell phone in it. He made it clear that my
pockets needed to be empty. I did as he said. At that time, two other guys
arrived, and a third followed a few minutes later, and I figured they were
in the same situation as me. John Bologna was the guy who had contacted
me to come to the city, and I had known him for years as an associate of
the Genovese crime family. The Genovese family was considered the most
powerful family in the country, and I was about to become a part of it.

The four of us sat at the table in silence. We had greeted each other at first but didn't talk about why we were there or what would take place that day. Joe and two other guys huddled across the room, whispering among themselves. I recognized one of them as Stevie Alfisi, a captain with the family, and the other was a soldier I didn't know. All three were dressed in custom-made suits, gold watches, and expensive jewelry. Many successful wiseguys prided themselves on being dressed to kill. In addition, a few others enjoyed the comfort of a sweatsuit—many wore both.

Once they finished talking, Joe came over and told me to come with him, and we left the restaurant. He took me to his car, and we drove a couple of blocks to an apartment building, a discreet social club where some wiseguys would go to drink and play cards. We went inside, and Joe led me to a small bathroom, where he told me to strip naked. I was to knock on the door when I finished. After knocking, he opened the door and asked for my clothes and shoes. He quickly glanced at my bare frame, handed me a white robe, and told me to put it on. I knew this protocol was to ensure I was not wearing a wire. The only place I could have hidden a wire that day was up my ass. That would have created some severe discomfort and possibly some serious internal complications. I understood that even though most wiseguys weren't afraid of too many things, the thought of being taped terrified us all. The Genovese family took such preventive measures for one reason—to protect themselves from being exposed to law enforcement. Being extremely careful is why they remained the most powerful of the five families.

As I sat on the toilet, waiting to become straightened out, and become a Made guy, my mind began to drift back to another time and place. It was the main reason I ended up in this bathroom.

▼ ▼ ▼

Arthur "Artie" Nigro had become a boss of the Genovese family, along with Larry Dentico and Mario Gigante. They were a panel of three who were the shot callers for the family. They assumed the positions after Ernie Muscarella got sentenced to five years in prison for extortion and racketeering. Muscarella had been moved up to become the boss, replacing the infamous Vincent "The Chin" Gigante, who faked insanity by walking around the city streets in a bathrobe and acting incoherently. Gigante was ultimately unsuccessful and ended up getting twelve years in prison. All these mobsters had once been top dogs in the East Harlem 116th Street Crew.

I was summoned to New York to meet with Artie; this was a big deal—he was a boss. After arriving, he told me he wanted me to take care of a guy named Frank Dadabo, a connected cement union steward he'd had a falling out with. Dadabo had been a friend of Artie's, and they spent time together going to fancy dinners and ballgames. But Artie was unhappy when Dadabo began running with the Lucchese family and sharing union contracts with them. The last straw was when Dadabo gave Tony Bennett tickets to a Lucchese guy that he had promised Artie. For this, he wanted Dadabo dead. All the good times and laughs they had shared didn't matter anymore. But this is how it is when you're in the game; it's usually your closest friend who's the one to clip you.

I had all the information I needed on Dadabo, including his photograph and most important his home address in the Bronx. Artie had given me two .22 caliber semi-automatic handguns with silencers for the hit, and I figured I needed two additional guys to do the job. One would wait in a getaway car while the other pulled the trigger along with me. Artie told me to use two Springfield guys who were already on the list to become Made members. Joey Basille and Reno Ceravalo were guys I knew, and although I trusted Reno, I didn't trust Joey—he was shaky. When I approached Joey about the job, he didn't want to do it and wanted to be taken off the list to become a Made guy. Joey wanted out of the game, and this didn't sit well with Artie, and he wanted to kill him. He told me to tell Joey to keep his mouth shut about the hit and not come around anymore—he was banished from interacting with any connected guys. Reno said he was willing to do the hit, but I could tell he really wasn't into it. I found out that he was apprehensive because he was confused by too many wiseguys he was dealing with, including Felix Tranghese, Al Bruno, Anthony Delevo, and Baba Scibelli. Reno didn't know who to believe or trust but said that he trusted me and that's why he agreed. In the end, I decided to let him walk away. I told Artie I didn't need him because I already had two other guys I trusted, and they were very capable of doing the job. I liked Reno and didn't want him to fall into the same fate as Joey, so we shook hands, and I could see that a weight was taken off his shoulders—he wasn't a killer.

Freddy and Ty Geas were two brothers I had known for years. I'm confident these guys would have become Made members if they had been born of Italian descent. Even though these brothers were natural-born killers, they were Greek, so they could never be more than Mob associates. I worked with both on robberies, extortion, and drug dealing, and I trusted them. When I approached them on the Dadabo hit, they accepted without apprehension or delay, and we got to work.

I planned to begin practicing with the two guns Artie had given us, so we went to the woods and set up targets. First, we lined up large bottles filled with water, then me and Ty chambered rounds while Freddy watched.

"It's hard to get a clear sight with these fuckin' silencers," Ty said as he turned toward me.

"Hey, stupid, point that thing away from me before you fuckin' shoot me," I said.

"Don't worry. I wouldn't shoot you unless it was on purpose," Ty said pointing the barrel back downrage.

"You crazy bastard, you probably would shoot me," I said, thinking one day he might. Ty wasn't wrapped too tightly, and he was paranoid, always thinking someone was out to get him. This made him extremely dangerous.

"Let's go. I hope you two clowns don't take this long to start shooting when we're doing the job," Freddy said.

Ty looked at his older brother and said, "Not too smart talking shit when we're holding loaded guns, and you're not."

"You'd probably miss me anyway, and then I'd take them from you and kick your asses," Freddy said with a smirk.

We didn't know it then, but Freddy would go on to be charged in the murder of Whitey Bulger while serving a life sentence at Hazelton Penitentiary in West Virginia.

Artie Nigro, center, and Frank Dabado

Ty began shooting, and after I started, we realized we needed to bridge the gap because we weren't hitting anything but dirt. After moving ten feet closer, I hit the first plastic bottle, causing a minimal explosion, and water began flowing out while the bottle remained standing. After a couple of shots, Ty hit his target, and then we had a line of success. I engaged a new clip and handed my gun to Freddy, and he aimed and started rapid firing. When he stopped, the bottle remained intact.

"Son of a bitch!" Freddy said as he quickly walked downrage to his target. He stopped, hovering over his bottle, steadying his barrel, and began shooting holes into it. "I killed the motherfucker," he yelled.

Me and Ty began laughing. "Okay, then," I said. "I think we know who'll wait in the getaway car."

"What?" Freddy said. "This is how close we'll be when we shoot him. I got this."

"That's alright," I said. "You're a much better driver than us. We will kill him, you drive."

"Okay, but you better not miss, or you'll never hear the end of it," Freddy said. I knew he was right, so we stayed and practiced for another hour.

Freddy had borrowed a relative's car, and a week later, we sat outside Dadabo's apartment doing a dry run. Around six in the morning, Dadabo entered his Cadillac just as Artie said he would. It was still somewhat dark, with the dawn beginning to peek its head up to start a new day. It was a perfect time to kill him—if we only had the guns and stolen plates on the car. Dadabo drove away and headed to work, not knowing that three killers were watching him and planning to take his life.

▼ ▼ ▼

The next day we drove from Springfield to the Bronx, leaving around two in the morning. On the way we stopped at a hotel in New Haven and stole a license plate, using a magnet to attach it to the back of the same car we used on the stakeout. Once we arrived outside Dadabo's apartment, we hid the guns under the car and waited for him to surface. On the way down, we planned the escape route and where to dispose of the guns and stolen plate. Now, it was just a matter of waiting for Dadabo to surface. Me and Ty were going to be the trigger men, while Freddy warmed the car seat, just as we had planned. We brought baseball caps to pull down, concealing the upper part of our faces. We didn't think we needed to wear sunglasses because it was still dark at six in the morning.

As the sun began to rise, we figured we fucked up and realized that wearing sunglasses would've been shrewd. The longer we waited, my adrenaline level lessened as more people started to appear on the street—there was no sign of Dadabo. He was a no-show. Around seven-thirty, we drove back to Springfield, disappointed and maybe even relieved. After all, taking the life of another person can be stressful, especially when you don't know him personally. If he had done something bad against us or a family member, it would be different.

Two days later, we did the drive again. This time, Freddy left the night before in the getaway car with the guns, and he checked into a hotel in Port Chester, New York. Ty and I drove down in my mother's car, and we met Freddy outside the hotel. We attached the stolen plate to the getaway car, leaving my mother's car behind.

For the third time, we waited outside Dadabo's apartment, expecting him to come out. It was May 19, 2003. This time, we hid the guns in the bushes, and I sat on a bench with Ty while Freddy waited in the car up the street.

"I gotta take a piss," Ty said. He got up and walked over to the bushes to do his business.

"What the fuck are you doing?" I asked.

"What?" He glanced over his shoulder.

"You're pissing right near the guns," I said. "Probably pissing on them."

"I'm not pissing on them; they're over there." He gestured with his head as his hands were clutching his pecker.

"What are you, an idiot?" I asked. "You're pissing all over a crime scene. What if the cops go through this area with their forensics team? Your DNA will be all over the place."

"Really?" Ty said. "You think they'll do that?" he asked as he zipped up and darted back to the bench.

"You better hope they don't," I said, busting balls.

As Ty sat back on the bench, I spotted Dadabo walking out of his apartment. "There he is," I said. "Let's get the guns."

Armed with the two pistols, we quickly moved toward his parked car, watching him get in and start the engine. When we reached his driver's side window, he turned and looked directly at us. The last thing Dadabo saw that morning was Ty and me standing two feet away, wearing dark clothes and hats, and pointing guns at him.

Before his first cup of coffee had kicked in, Dadabo sat slumped over, covered in blood. The muffled sound of the gunshots and the shattered window didn't appear to alarm anyone as we pumped nine rounds into him. I looked at Ty and we both figured he was dead, and Freddy came shuffling over to see.

"He's dead," Freddy said.

We ran back down the street and jumped into the car and drove off.

A few miles away, we stopped on a bridge overlooking marsh wetlands; we switched plates, tossed the guns and stolen plate over the railing, and drove away. As we traveled up the street, I used scissors to cut the two hats into small pieces and threw them out the window.

After arriving back at the hotel, we jumped back into my mother's car, and me and Ty headed back to Springfield. We met Freddy at his West Springfield apartment and washed our hands with our piss. I had watched a show on TV where some guys did this to eliminate any handgun residue. I did some research later and read that vinegar was also a good solution, but urine was better.

One thing that bothered me about shooting Dadabo was that we wouldn't get street cred for the hit. When you're in the life, it's a good thing to have a murder under your belt to gain respect and fear on the streets. We wouldn't get that because the only ones who knew about the hit were Artie Nigro, John Bologna, and us. And that's the way it had to stay. Nobody else could ever know that we had anything to do with what happened in the Bronx that morning.

The next day, Bologna called and told me that Dadabo was still alive. We should have learned a lesson that day—use a high-caliber gun, not a twenty-two, and aim for the head. All nine shots went into his body, and Dadabo later said he was covering his head while being shot, thinking he could survive if he avoided a head shot.

▼ ▼ ▼

Finally, there was a knock on the bathroom door. I opened it, and Joe told me to follow him. We entered a room where Artie, Pat, Steve, and Ralph were waiting. I felt awkward being naked under the light robe they gave me as we all stood around a table. A gun and knife was placed on the table in front of me.

"Do you know why you're here?" Nigro asked.

"No." Bologna had told me why I was summoned to New York, but he said I wasn't supposed to know and to act surprised.

"You've been asked here today because you have proven yourself on the street and shown you are trustworthy."

I figured every man in the room had killed someone in order to be standing with me. It was a room full of murderers. And even though Dadabo didn't die, they knew I intended to kill him. It was only an act of God that saved him.

"You are being inducted to become a member of our secret society. To become a part of this thing of ours," Nigro said. "To become a part of our family."

"I understand."

"Do you understand that this family of ours comes first and foremost? That our family comes before your wife and kids?"

"Yes."

"If you're in the hospital with your wife, who is giving birth to your son, and we call on you for a meeting, you must leave the hospital immediately. Will you do that?"

"Yes."

"This thing of ours, Cosa Nostra, has a chain of command and has rules. You must follow the chain of command, and you must follow the rules." Nigro said. "Will you obey the chain of command and our rules?"

"Yes, I will."

"You are to never deal in narcotics. You are not to get involved with counterfeit money. You must never lay your hands on another Made member. And you don't touch another Made member's family. Do you understand and agree to these rules?"

"Yes," I lied. I was pretty sure I would violate the narcotics rule.

"You should never talk to anyone about this thing of ours. Do you understand?"

"Yes."

Nigro produced a pin and Pat had a lighter and a piece of tissue paper with Saint Francis inscribed on it. "Give me your hand," Nigro said.

I reached out, offering my hand.

"We live by the gun and the knife." He pricked my finger, and blood began to surface, then he squeezed my finger. I watched as my blood dripped onto the tissue Pat was holding. "Cup your hands," Nigro commanded.

I did as I was told, and Pat lit the bloody tissue, and as it burned in my hands, Nigro spoke again.

"You must adhere to the vow of omertà. The vow of silence."

"Do you know what this means?"

"Yes."

"If you ever break your vow of omertà, your soul will burn like this tissue. Do you understand?"

"Yes."

"Do you swear to obey this vow of omertà?"

"Yes, I do."

"Welcome to our family." Artie Nigro moved in and kissed me on both cheeks. "Gentlemen, say hello to a friend of ours."

The other four guys kissed me on the cheeks, and then we all shook hands as they welcomed me into the family. Getting made by the actual boss of the New York family was a big deal. The captain of Springfield made most guys from that city, but I was directly under the power of New York, which put me at an entirely different level.

After I got dressed, we returned to the Nebraska Steak House, where we had drinks and dinner. I was in my glory. I was now a Made guy in the Genovese crime family. I had the power, and I was untouchable. It was time to build my empire.

MAKING OF
A MOBSTER

CHAPTER 2

Looking back, my life as a troublemaker and criminal began when I was about eight or nine. I was born in the Six Corners section of Springfield, but I hung around the South End. Many Italians lived in the South End, and Main Street cut right through the middle of the neighborhood. Later, we moved to East Springfield to live with my grandmother, about five and a half miles away. However, after we moved, I continued at Mount Carmel School in the South End. I commuted by bus or took a ride when I could get one. All my friends lived there, and like me, they were Italian.

At the time, the boss of our area was "Big Nose" Sam Cufari, a captain in the Genovese crime family out of New York. To all who knew Sam, he was the boss. He controlled or had a stake in many cities including Springfield and Worcester, Massachusetts; Hartford and New Haven, Connecticut; and Albany, New York.

Me and my best friend Anthony Scibelli were little wiseguys. We were around nine years old when we started skipping school and hanging out around coffee shops and restaurants down the South End. We spent our days playing arcade games with money the goodfellas gave us. The main joints we hung out at were Ciro's Restaurant, Gennaro's, La Fiorentina Pastry Shop, and a few other places. We didn't know it at the time, but the adults who hung around there were Made Mafia guys like; "Big Al" Bruno, "Skyball" Scibelli, "Baba" Scibelli, Anthony Delevo, and other members of the Genovese family. We saw them as tough, knockaround guys, but they treated us well. Like them, we were Italian, and we were from the neighborhood.

Donny Pepe was the driver for Big Nose Sam, and at the time, he was dating my Aunt Grace Siano. Donny used to hang around the same places we would go to after school or when we played hooky. He would often give me money to play with the machines, and sometimes, he would give me a ride home after school. Donny hung around our house to spend time with Grace—he was like one of the family.

As time went on, I went from playing arcade games to betting on football and baseball games. When we weren't betting on games, Anthony Scibelli, Ralphie Santaniello, me, and some other neighborhood kids were getting into fights regularly.

I started taking bets from friends and kids at school using football tickets. Back in the Seventies and Eighties, football tickets were huge. The minimum bet was a buck; you had to pick at least four teams. To win, you had to get four out of four, but the more games you picked, the more money you would win. There were no limits to how much money you could bet. When I was nine, my mother found a bundle of tickets with a slip of paper detailing who owed me money and who I had to pay off—she went ballistic.

I used to get football tickets from Donny, and I was at a point where I was making serious money for a kid in the seventh grade. I was personally betting a hundred bucks a game, and my football ticket customers were growing. I was even taking bets from my seventh-grade teacher, who was friends with my Uncle Mike Siano. She went to a bar he hung out at, and she became a regular customer with the football tickets.

As a teen, I would hang around the Our Lady of Grace Italian club, Mount Carmel Society and the Assunta Club. We would also play basketball at the Howard Street Recreation Center, and we ended up getting into gang fights there on several occasions. Me and my friends were rumbling with the Black, Puerto Rican, and Irish kids, and by then we had graduated to using weapons. I was never the biggest or the toughest kid, but I wasn't afraid to use a weapon to win the day, and that caught up with me quickly. When I was about fifteen, I was arrested for assault and battery with a dangerous weapon. We got into a fight with a bunch of kids at Allen and Cooley Street, and I hit a kid over the head with a broomstick with a nail sticking out of it. I was lucky that time because I won the court case on appeal.

By the time I was sixteen, I was betting five thousand a game. I was still taking bets on football tickets, but I was also making direct bets with a bookie who worked for Rex Cunningham. Rex was a local bar owner whose uncle was Mario Fiore, and he was connected. After a rough streak, I was down seventy-seven thousand dollars, and only had thirty thousand on hand. I was at home when the phone rang.

"Hello."

"Bingy."

"Yeah." Bingy was my nickname.

"This is Rex. Where's my money?"

"I don't have it right now, but I'll get it to you."

"When?" His voice was impatient and angry.

"Give me a week or two."

"No. I want my fucking money *now*."

"I'll get it to you; just give me some time."

"You're already late, you little cocksucker. You have until tomorrow."

I went silent. I didn't like the way he was talking to me. I wanted to kill him.

"Did you hear what I said?"

"Yeah."

"Seventy-seven large—tomorrow."

"Right." The phone went dead.

I knew Rex wasn't a guy to take lightly. In 1998 he was sentenced to seventeen years in federal prison after being caught on a wiretap bragging about how he followed a guy who owed him money on an unpaid loan to his sister's wake and broke his arm. In addition to assault and battery, Rex was convicted of racketeering, extortion, and illegal gambling.

▼ ▼ ▼

My father owned a successful produce store on Bay Street, and the wiseguys would use the back room for meetings. To be clear, my father was a legitimate businessman, but had many connections with Mob guys. He used to play golf with Bruno and would go out to dinner with some of the other Made guys, but besides betting on sports games, he was clean. Once or twice a week they would meet at his store, and I would see them coming and going while I was working. I used to help out stacking shelves and sweeping the floor.

My father told my mother about my situation, and my mother, being friends with Anthony Delevo's wife, told her about the money I owed Rex. Anthony Delevo was a soldier at the time, and he carried a lot of weight in the city—especially with the boss, Skyball Scibelli.

The next day, I was told to meet Delevo at my father's store, and that afternoon, I showed up.

"Hey, pop," I said as I walked into the store.

"He's in the back. Keep your cool," my father warned.

I walked into the back room to find Delevo sitting in wait. He just sat staring at me with burning eyes that seared through my pupils. Finally, he got up and walked over to me, and the next thing I felt was a slap—it stung.

"You little shit. What the fuck are you doing placing bets for thousands of dollars?"

"I'm sorry. It got out of hand," I said.

"You're sorry?" He slapped me again, this time harder. "Do you know what kind of a position you've put me in? I should break both your fucking legs."

Go ahead, and I'll come back with a gun and blow your head off, I thought.

"Where did you get the money to bet? Is your father in on this?"

"No. He has nothing to do with this."

Another slap. Now I was getting pissed. I wanted to kill Delevo.

"How much do you have?"

"Thirty thousand."

"That makes you short forty-seven thousand. Where the fuck are you going to get that kind of money?"

"I'll make it back on Sunday's games."

Wrong answer. I saw Delevo's eyes go dead, and he reached out, grabbed me by the throat, pinned me against the wall, and he slapped me two more times.

"You'll do what?"

"Okay, I'll stop betting."

He let go. "You bet your ass you'll stop betting. You better have a serious talk with your father. You need to find a way to come up with the scratch soon."

"Okay, I will."

*My father and
me in 1986*

He walked out. I looked in the mirror; my face was beet-red and still stinging. I seriously wanted to kill him.

When Al Bruno found out, he went to see Rex and scolded him for taking bets from a sixteen-year-old kid. Rex responded by saying he thought I was taking bets for my father. In the end, Al worked out a deal with Rex and had ten grand taken off my debt. My father came up with the other thirty-seven thousand, and I was warned not to bet games anymore, but I continued to place bets, just not with Rex. I wasn't happy with how the whole thing went down, especially how they treated my father and me. I was furious because of this, and I wanted to kill Bruno too.

▼ ▼ ▼

Around the same time, I started taking trips down to Port St. Lucie with my Uncle Mike. He was my mother's brother and had never worked a day in his life. His entire existence involved hustling on the streets. He's a guy with no education, never graduated from high school, yet he thought he knew everything—a real Mr. Know-It-All.

Uncle Mike had this bright idea that if he traveled with a kid, the cops would look past him as he trafficked cocaine from Florida to Massachusetts. We would fly down and meet with Jerry, a friend of the family, buy a couple of keys of coke and drive it back up north hidden in a spare tire in the trunk. Uncle Mike would buy old cars for around five grand, and we would drive them back home with the drugs hidden in the back.

For me, it was like a vacation. My aunt lived down there, and I'd stay at her place, and she would cook some delicious meals. She was a great cook. I used to hang out at the beach and occasionally go swimming at Jerry's house. I enjoyed our trips to Florida, and I knew exactly what my uncle was up to. I would overhear them talking about the coke, and one time, I saw the bundles all packaged up and ready for sale.

We must have made a half dozen trips while I was sixteen and seventeen years old, and sometimes Donny Pepe's cousin Sonny would come along. He was a halfwit cokehead who was constantly filling his nose with the white powder. One positive thing I'll say about my Uncle Mike is that he didn't take drugs—he just sold them.

At one point, the FBI had Donny on its radar. He was hiding out at my aunt's place in Florida, which seemed to be where many guys on the lam stayed. Another guy, named Red Boulder, was also wanted by the FBI for robbing banks, and he was there as well.

Here I am, not even an adult yet, and I'm involved in trafficking cocaine and hanging out with fugitives wanted by the FBI—this isn't how a sixteen-year-old is supposed to spend his time.

▼ ▼ ▼

A few weeks before Christmas of 1985, it all came tumbling down. I was in the back seat of my uncle's shiny, old Ford that he had bought before heading home. Sonny was in the passenger seat snorting coke like he had to fill his empty forehead.

"You keep sniffing that shit, and your nose is going to fall off," I said.

"You just sit back there and shut up," he said with a grunt.

"You shut the fuck up, you idiot. You're going to get us arrested."

"Mike, tell your nephew to shut the fuck up," Sonny said.

He glanced back at me. "Anthony, be quiet."

We stopped at a convenience store to buy some drinks and snacks and take a piss. Shortly afterward, we were heading north when cruiser lights lit up our car. My uncle pulled over. A Maryland State Trooper approached the vehicle, and Sonny took his stash out and hid it in the car.

"License and registration, please," said a tall, serious-looking trooper with a large scar defining his cheek.

He looked at the documents. "You just bought this car?"

"Yes," Mike said, maintaining his composure.

"Where are you heading?"

"Home, Massachusetts. We were visiting family in Florida, and I thought I should buy this car."

Mike was acting cool, but Sonny appeared nervous.

"How old are you?" He asked me.

"Seventeen."

"Okay, I want you to step out of the car."

I did as he ordered, and he put me in the back seat of his police cruiser. I watched as he took Sonny out, brought him to his car, and placed him in the front seat. The trooper then ordered my uncle out of the car and began patting him down, as he had also done with us. After that he began searching inside the car, and a minute later, he found Sonny's bag of coke under the seat, and off to jail we went.

They had the car impounded. After thoroughly searching the car, the cops found two kilos of cocaine inside a tire. Mike and Sonny were both charged with trafficking in narcotics, and I was released to my parent's custody because I was still considered a juvenile.

When I got back home, the arrest was all over the newspapers. Even though my name wasn't released, everyone knew I got arrested with Mike and Sonny. I was big-time now and was getting street cred and respect from my neighborhood friends.

A couple of days later, on December 16, 1985, Gambino boss Paul Castellano was shot to death in front of Sparks Steak House in Manhattan. John Gotti was the mastermind behind the hit.

Castellano's murder was big news and was broadcast all over the television and was printed on the front page of most national newspapers. At that time, I knew I wanted to be in the life—the life of a mobster.

For the cocaine trafficking arrest, my Uncle Mike got sentenced to five years in prison, and Sonny Pepe received one year. I was a juvenile, acted ignorant, and got off with a slap on the wrist. I now had a reputation on the streets.

Soon after the arrest, my crew of friends and I were getting into a lot of fights in local bars. Most of the bars were owned by wiseguys from the South End, and we were pissing off quite a few of them. Even though we were all underage, we had fake IDs, and in many cases we knew the owners of the bars. After a while I was getting bounced out of most of the bars downtown, and I was running out of places to drink and hang out.

The day me and my boys graduated from fighting with pipes, bats, and knives to using guns happened at a bar called Ten Years After. There were around six of us, including my best friend, Anthony Scibelli. The fight started inside and ended up on the street, with the six of us battling it out with seven guys from Holyoke. As we tangled in the street, I noticed a Black guy standing on the sideline holding a hatchet. I wasn't sure if he was with anyone because the guys we were fighting against were all white. In an instant, the Black guy ran up to Anthony and hit him over the head with the sharp end of the hatchet. Anthony fell to his knees, blood pouring from his head like a punctured hose. At that point, I went after the guy, but the cops swarmed the scene, he ran away, and I lost him.

Somebody took Anthony to the emergency room, and I followed him down there. After waiting outside the emergency room for a while, I was told he was going to be okay, so I went home. Around four in the morning, my mother came into my bedroom and woke me up.

"Anthony isn't doing well," she said as she stood in the doorway. "The blade was buried deep into his head, and he suffered a fractured skull."

"What?" I sat up, cleaning the sleep out of my eyes.

"You better head down there. He may not make it."

I couldn't believe what I was hearing. My best friend might die. I raced to the hospital, and after several hours of surgery, the doctor said they had to put a steel plate in his head. He said Anthony was fortunate but that he would be fragile for weeks. Any hard pressure against the plate could kill him. I was so relieved he was going to live. And then my relief turned to anger.

For several days, around twenty guys from our gang and I patrolled the streets of Holyoke, looking inside bars and asking some hard questions. We had a few cars filled with guys, and we kept going back for weeks, looking for the guy who almost killed my friend. This time was different from the past because I had a handgun, and I was planning to kill him. Around four months went by, and I finally got a tip about where the guy hung out, so me and two friends headed to Holyoke to check it out. After arriving, I went inside because I could identify him from the night of the brawl. I walked into the bar unarmed, leaving my gun in the car. After less than a minute, I spotted him sitting at the bar, and I went back out, and we waited in the car for him to come out. A couple of hours later, he surfaced.

"Give me the gun," I said to my friend. (I can't divulge his name because the case is still open.)

"No, let me kill this, guy," he said as he gripped the gun.

"Are you sure?"

"Yes," he said without hesitation and with a crazy glare in his eye.

He got out of the car and quickly approached the guy as he was getting into his car. "This is for Anthony," he said. Then, he shot the guy three times.

In an instant, we were gone and headed back to Springfield. A couple of days later, we saw on the news that the guy we shot was in critical condition but expected to live. There were no suspects. We never heard anything about the shooting again—nobody came looking for any of us.

▼ ▼ ▼

In the early summer of 1992, I was on parole for carrying an unregistered handgun and shooting a firearm out of a moving vehicle. I was at Tiffany's bar talking to a beautiful young lady when one of our guys, Gerald Daniele, came storming in. He had a very rocky relationship with his girlfriend Gina Garafolo. He had slapped her around a few times in the past, and she told her brothers. Tensions were running high between them for a while, and it came to a boiling point that night, and he got into a fight with a couple of her brothers. Gerald was one of us, so six of us jumped into a car and drove to Gina's grandmother's house in the Sixteen Acres section of Springfield.

Joe Garafolo was one of her brothers and he was a Springfield police officer. When we arrived at the house, we got out of the car, and I had an ax handle at the ready. Gina's brother Joe came onto the front lawn to check things out, and then he slowly walked back into the house. I followed him inside and hit him with a good shot to the head with my club, splitting his head wide-open. The force of the blow broke the ax handle, so I began stabbing him in the stomach with the sharp wooden edge. Once the cop was out of commission, we beat down everyone else in the house.

A few minutes later, we heard the sirens, so we jumped back in the car and took off. As we drove away, the cruisers were passing by us. I figured it was just a matter of time before they pulled us over. After all, I just beat up a cop. At that point, I suggested we ditch the car and flee on foot, and, luckily, we all managed to get away.

I figured the cops would come looking for us, and I had the most to lose because I was on parole. I'd be facing a home-invasion charge and assault and battery on a police officer with a dangerous weapon inside a dwelling. If convicted, I was looking at some serious time. Violating my parole meant that I would immediately end up back in the can. The days turned into weeks, and we didn't hear a thing. No police, no indictments, and no summons to appear in court. It turned out that Gerald and Gina had reconciled, and Bruno knew someone in the Garafolo family, and he convinced them not to press charges or pursue any retribution for the attack.

Right after the incident occurred, my attorney Bobby Santaniello suggested that I find an alibi, so I went to the Hu Ke Lau Chinese restaurant in Chicopee to see Johnny Yee, the manager. I was sitting at a table with a couple of friends when Johnny came over.

"Anthony, how are you?" Johnny said.

"I'm good, Johnny, and you?"

"Good."

I stood up and shook his hand. "Johnny, can I have a minute?"

"Sure."

Johnny was a solid guy. He liked to be known as someone with deep connections with the Mob. So when a wiseguy went to Johnny's place, he treated them like royalty.

"I could use your help," I said as we walked away from the table.

"Sure, what can I do?" Johnny said with a serious look.

"Two nights ago, I was here having dinner on Thursday, remember?"

Johnny hesitated for a few seconds. "Yes, I remember. You were here all night. We had dinner, and then you and I drank cognac until we closed the place." Johnny patted me on the shoulder. "We had a great time, Thursday."

I laughed. "We really did have a great time. Johnny, would you be willing to sign an affidavit stating this?"

"Of course I would," Jonny said with a smile.

"Great. I won't forget this, Johnny. My attorney Bobby Santaniello will be in touch. Now, let's get some drinks for my friends and me. These were the same two guys that were with us Thursday night."

"Yes, I remember them too," he said with a grin.

"Thanks, Johnny."

Three months later, Gerald and Gina had another huge fight, and she went to the DA and told him all about the home invasion and assault. I had thought this whole ordeal was behind us, but I was wrong. It made me think of the old saying my father had told me: "Hell hath no fury like a woman scorned."

The entire crew was arrested, and I turned myself in. I was arraigned and held without bail, and the other guys were out on bail pending trial. I was shipped off to Concord, and soon after, Gerald and Gina were back on good terms and engaged to be married.

In the end, I beat the case because the witnesses were reluctant to testify, and I had a solid alibi. I went in front of the parole board, and Mike Albano, who sat on the board, was the deciding vote. Fortunately, Albano, who would become Mayor of Springfield, was connected to the Mob and voted in my favor.

I felt like the luckiest son of a bitch in the world. I was looking at doing at least ten years in prison—maybe more—and I got off unscathed. This would be a trend I would enjoy most of my life, especially when facing death by lethal injection.

OLD TIME WISEGUYS

CHAPTER 3

The Genovese family has had roots in the Greater Springfield area for over a century. This includes Hartford, New Haven, Bridgeport, Worcester, and Albany. As time evolved, the Patriarca family out of Providence, Rhode Island, would come to share New Haven, Bridgeport, and Worcester with the Genovese family.

Many wiseguys controlling these cities grew up in Springfield, and the legacy of criminal activity and corruption still lives on. Generations of Fiores, Scibellis, Santaniellos, and Albanos are still allegedly connected to the Costa Nostra today.

Former Springfield Mayor Michael J. Albano served eight years as mayor, and, at the end of his tenure, his family name and legacy revealed its ugly face. In 2001, the FBI began investigating illegal activity and corruption surrounding the mayor's office. It ended with over thirty indictments, including Albano's Chief of Staff, Anthony Ardolino, and Albano-appointed Springfield Police Commissioner, Gerald Phillips. Both were convicted and served time in federal prison. But speculation that Albano cooperated with the feds to avoid indictment was widespread. Although Albano denied being connected to the Italian Mafia, one of his biggest campaign contributors was Emilio Fusco, a Made member of the Genovese crime family. One of the ongoing questions has been "Did the

Mob come to Springfield because the politicians were corrupt or did the Mob corrupt the politicians?"

▼ ▼ ▼

Pasqualina Albano was named "Bootlegging Queen of Little Italy" in Springfield during the early 1920s until she was killed in a drive-by shooting in 1932. She is a relative of Michael Albano, the former mayor of Springfield. Her husband, Carlo Siniscalchi, had been running the most extensive bootlegging operation in the Greater Springfield area until he was shot to death by Guiseppi Parisi in Springfield in 1921, while he sat in his limousine waiting for a cigar.

After the death of her husband, Pasqualina took over the operation. A couple of years later, Pasqualina married Antonio Miranda, a guy from New York who was an associate of Frank Costello, Lucky Luciano, and Vito Genovese. These mobsters worked under Joe "The Boss" Masseria and were involved in bootlegging, extortion, gambling, prostitution, and murder. These connections were how the Genovese family started its working relationships with organized criminals in the Springfield area.

Miranda died of blood poisoning in 1930 due to complications from minor surgery. Pasqualina continued the operation with her right-hand man Michael Fiore until November 12, 1932. On that cold Saturday morning, a black sedan approached while Pasqualina and Michael sat in his car on Worthington Street. Killers with machine guns and a shotgun opened fire from a sedan killing Pasqualina and wounding Fiore in the arm. No one was ever apprehended.

Fiore had a history of violence, including stabbing a Springfield Police Officer and the attempted murder of a man in Connecticut. He was shot to death five months after Pasqualina was killed while getting his hair cut at a Springfield barbershop.

▼ ▼ ▼

Vito Genovese had fled to Italy to avoid prosecution for the murder of Ferdinand Boccia in 1937. After the war ended, he returned to New York, where he assumed the title "Boss" of the family. Soon afterward, he inducted "Big Nose Sam" Cufari into the family, and in 1948, Sam took over as captain of the Greater Springfield faction of the Genovese family.

Sam had several soldiers in his crew, including Al Bruno, Felix Tranghese, and Skyball Scibelli. Ironically, Scibelli's family was from, Quindici, Italy, the same village where Carlo Siniscalchi had grown up.

Ralph "Whitey" Tropiano ran the New Haven operation in the late Fifties and Sixties. Tropiano was a serious wiseguy who was said to be part of the infamous "Murder Inc." hit squad run by Albert Anastasia in the late Thirties. As a member of the Colombo family, Tropiano reportedly killed scores of people. He was arrested in the late Forties for two murders, but the charges were dropped without an explanation. Over the next two years, over a dozen members of his crew turned up dead in the streets of Brooklyn. It was widely accepted on the streets that Tropiano was responsible for the murders. Tropiano's boss told him to eliminate his crew, or he would be taken out because his crew was caught stealing from Mafia gambling operations. Tropiano was never brought to justice for the murders because he paid a New York homicide detective twenty-thousand dollars to kill an eyewitness that a district attorney had taken a statement from.

On October 4, 1951, while having lunch with Willie Morelli, the New Jersey boss of the Genovese family, it was said that Tropiano shot him to death because he had testified in front of the Kefauver Commission. Tropiano's reward for the hit was that he could assume control of New Haven, Connecticut.

Tropiano's murderous rampage continued after he left New York. In 1962 the bullet-riddled body of Thomas "Pinocchio" Rispoli was found buried in the basement of an abandoned home in Branford, just outside of New Haven. Two weeks earlier, Rispoli had punched Tropiano in the face over a gaming dispute. It is believed he paid the ultimate price for taking that swing.

During his reign, Tropiano mentored a local up-and-comer named William "Wild Guy" Grasso, a member of the Patriarca crime family in Rhode Island. Grasso had been cellmates with the boss, Raymond Patriarca, and they formed a bond while serving time. Grasso was a no-nonsense guy who didn't drink alcohol or smoke and he didn't want anyone around him to partake either. His reputation for having a short temper and treating his crew with disdain was well known. Grasso was a guy who was nasty to just about everyone, and he was hated by many and feared by most.

Danny Vitarelli was my uncle—my grandmother's brother. He was connected to the Genovese and Patriarca families and was a close associate of Tropiano, and they were good friends. Raymond Patriarca and Billy Grasso had a meeting and decided Tropiano had to go.

Grasso wanted to enjoy the spoils Tropiano was earning in the Greater New Haven area, and rumor had it that Tropiano was a government informant. Patriarca approached my Uncle Danny and told him he wanted him to kill Tropiano. As the pressure mounted, my uncle couldn't come to terms with betraying his longtime friend; so instead, he shot himself in the head. Tropiano narrowly escaped getting whacked.

Tropiano was sentenced to prison in the late Seventies for bribing a police officer. After his release, he and Grasso were engaged in a power struggle in New Haven, and in June of 1980, Tropiano was shot to death while walking down a street in Brooklyn, New York.

With Tropiano out of the picture, Grasso was now running New Haven, along with Genovese captain Salvatore "Midgie" Annunziato. Not only were they involved with loan-sharking, gambling, extortion, and bookmaking, but Grasso also had the Bridgeport waste-management business under his control. The two gangsters were also into boxing and controlled several fighters. They were fixing bouts at many New Haven, Norwich, Hartford, and Waterbury venues.

Patriarca was on the move and expanding his empire. After consolidating his operations in Providence, Boston, Worcester, Bridgeport, and New Haven, he set his sights on Springfield. But he learned that could cause serious problems with "Big Nose Sam" Cufari, so he backed off. Patriarca's biggest threat at the time was the Irish gangs out of Boston, notably the Winter Hill Gang, run by Whitey Bulger.

Vito Genovese

Sharing operations with the Genovese family was causing a lot of tension with Patriarca, and on June 19, 1979, Sal Annunziato disappeared after a meeting with Grasso. The following January, another Genovese associate, Tommy "The Blonde" Vastano, was shot to death in his backyard in Stratford, Connecticut.

Many mobsters were shot, blown up, and mysteriously disappearing in the Seventies and early Eighties. Most of these were linked to Billy "Wild Guy" Grasso.

Raymond Patriarca Sr. died of a sudden heart attack in 1984, and was succeeded by his son Raymond Patriarca Jr. After his friend and mentor died, Grasso started down a path of complete recklessness. The guys in Grasso's crew felt he was taking advantage of them because he was greedy and grabbing the bulk of all incoming cash. Grasso's crew was also afraid he would turn on them one day, and they might disappear like many others had.

In September of 1988, Grasso got into an argument with an amateur boxer, Eric Miller, on a busy corner of the South End in Hartford. After Grasso had threatened to cut Miller's eyes out with a knife, Miller got out of his car and Grasso came at him with the blade. Even though Grasso was tough, he was no match for a trained boxer. Miller knocked him out cold with a hard right to the face. Three months later, Miller was shot in the head and left to die on Ledyard Street in Hartford. Miller, a low-level coke dealer, should have known better than to lay hands on a Made guy—especially the underboss of the Patriarca family. Unfortunately, he paid dearly for his mistake. Even though there was subsequent testimony from Grasso associate John "Jackie" Johns that Grasso killed Miller, no charges were ever filed in the case.

Grasso, who was now making millions of dollars, was not content and he wanted more. He began threatening to make a move on the Springfield family, now run by Genovese captain Francesco "Skyball" Scibelli. Even though Scibelli was a little guy, he had a reputation of being ruthless and it wouldn't be an easy task trying to take over his territory. Grasso decided it was too bold a move and he didn't attempt the coup.

Grasso and his right-hand man from Boston, "Cadillac" Frank Salemme, began plotting to take over the Patriarca family. They considered Raymond Jr. to be a moron and a weak boss, who would also be an easy target. Salemme was close friends with Stevie "Rifleman" Flemmi, Whitey Bulger's top enforcer.

The crew operating out of the North End of Boston wanted both Grasso and Salemme gone, but first they had to get approval from the commission out of New York to kill Grasso. The violence and murders he was perpetrating, the alienation of his crew, and his plot to expand into other bosses' territories were causing dissension and drawing heat from law enforcement. Simply stated, Grasso's carelessness was bad for business, and something needed to be done quickly. John Gotti and the other bosses of the New York families knew what was happening up north, and they agreed Grasso's recklessness was out of control and they unanimously agreed Grasso had to go.

On June 13, 1989, Grasso agreed to a meeting to sort out the ongoing issues between the Springfield Crew and Providence. Gaetano Milano, a newly Made member of the Patriarca family who lived in West Springfield, arranged to pick up Grasso to attend a meeting in Worcester, Massachusetts. Grasso and Milano were both Made guys in the Patriarca family, so Grasso must have trusted he would be safe. They were going to meet with Carlo Mastrototaro, who ran Worcester, and he would act as a mediator to help work out the differences between Grasso and Scibelli of Springfield.

When they picked up Grasso in a van, Milano was with brothers Frank and Louis Pugliano, who were connected to the Genovese and Patriarca families. Also in the van was Frank Colantoni Jr., a Patriarca associate. As the van moved down the street, Milano, who was seated behind Grasso, shot him in the neck. They watched as blood poured out, soiling the van and Grasso took his last breath. Grasso's body was found three days later, dumped in a patch of poison ivy near the Connecticut River in Wethersfield, Connecticut.

Grasso's associate, Frank Salemme, who was also close with Whitey Bulger, was riddled with bullets on the same day Grasso was whacked as he walked out of an IHOP restaurant in Saugus, Massachusetts. He survived.

Once Grasso was out of the picture, things began to get back to normal, and the Springfield-based mob would continue their criminal activities without conflict. At least for a while.

The Patriarca family had been under federal investigation for a RICO case (Racketeer Influenced and Corrupt Organizations Act). As a result, around twenty mobsters were arrested in Boston and Connecticut. These arrests paved the way for the Springfield faction of the Genovese family to take over much of the Connecticut operation.

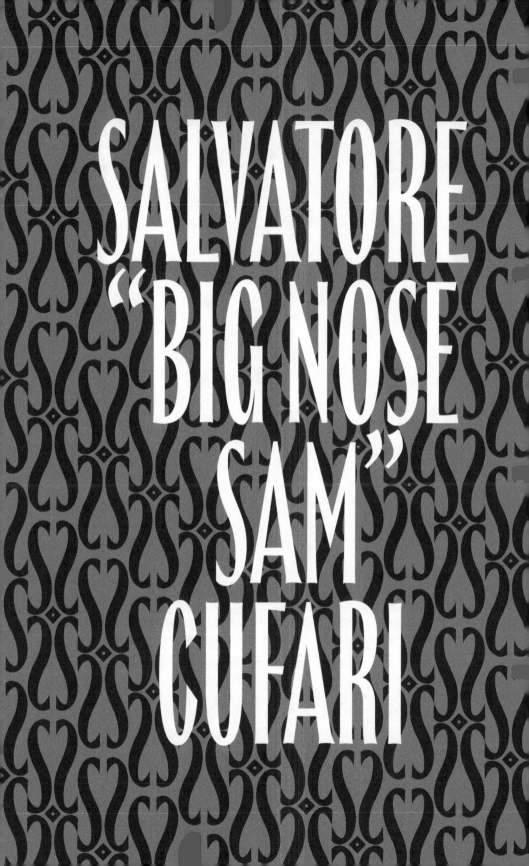

SALVATORE
"BIG NOSE
SAM"
CUFARI

CHAPTER 4

ooking back at all the bosses who ran the Mob in the Greater Springfield area since the beginning, Sam Cufari had the longest reign of any other capo. Sam was the guy in charge for thirty-five years. An important thing to remember is that he never spent any time in prison. A remarkable feat because nearly all the wiseguys I mentioned were in and out of prison most of their lives. Sam was smart because he kept a low profile and avoided serious and long-term conflicts with other mobsters and law enforcement. He was not a guy who lost control and flew off the handle or was directly connected to acts of violence, and he treated his crew well. Sam was also smart because he knew how to delegate. If someone needed to be dealt with, he'd give a nod to one of his loyal soldiers, and it was handled. Sam was also careful by surrounding himself with very loyal guys such as Skyball Scibelli. Scibelli was of the old school and could be trusted to abide by his vow of omertà.

Sam was a person who gained respect from other wiseguys, business leaders, politicians, judges, and some local law enforcement personnel. Keeping a low profile and a subdued demeanor helped him pave the way to building a criminal empire without the drama and exposure that would bring him to his knees.

▼ ▼ ▼

Salvatore "Big Nose Sam" Cufari was born on January 31, 1901, in Bianco, Reggio di Calabria, Italy. He emigrated to New York City in 1914. Ten years

Big Nose
Sam Cufari

later, he was arrested on Christmas Eve for stabbing a gas station attendant in Enfield, Connecticut. He was never charged with the crime because the victim wouldn't identify Sam as the assailant. The following year, Sam was injured in a police shootout—no charges were brought against him. This was a common theme with Sam; he had a way of slipping through the judicial cracks.

In the earlier days, Sam began his life of crime in New York as a bootlegger. This is where he developed his deep relationships with Vito Genovese, Frank Costello, and Charles "Lucky" Luciano. After Prohibition ended in December of 1933, however, Sam shifted his earning capabilities to loansharking, gambling, and extortion.

Soon after the war ended, Vito Genovese returned to America from Italy, and he took Sam under his wing. In 1948, Sam moved to Springfield as the captain of the Genovese family and maintained control over Springfield, Hartford, Albany, and Schenectady, and had some shared responsibility for New Haven and Bridgeport. He operated out of a small office on Main Street in the South End of Springfield. Sam also spent a lot of time at Ciro's Restaurant up the street, where he was a part owner. Even though most of his income was from illegal activity, he also had a stake in many legitimate businesses.

As a family man, married with two children, Sam thought it was important to maintain a profile within the community where he wasn't seen as a thug but as a community businessman who believed in the sanctity of family.

In 1957, Vito Genovese called for a national meeting of Mafia bosses to be held at Joseph Barbara's fifty-eight-acre estate in rural Apalachin, New York. He called for the meeting to discuss gambling, Mob operations at casinos, the New York garment industry, and the sale of narcotics, which was a growing enterprise. They also needed to discuss how they would divide the criminal empire that Albert Anastasia, now deceased, once operated. Tensions had run very high after the shotgun killing of Anastasia, who had once headed up the infamous "Murder Inc." hit squad (along with Lepke Buchalter). Also, on the same day as the Anastasia murder, Frank Costello survived an attempted hit.

A couple of loyalists to Anastasia, Aniello "Neal" Dellacroce and Armand "Tommy" Rava, were on the verge of war with the Genovese family because Vito had planned the hit on Anastasia, and he was moving to take control over the former Luciano family. Also on the agenda was the control of the gambling and narcotics operations on the island of Cuba, which concerned Meyer Lansky and his partners. Before Anastasia was killed, he attempted to muscle in on Lansky's operations, and they needed to ensure that Dellacroce and Rava understood that the island was off-limits.

New York State Trooper Edgar Croswell had been periodically watching the property of Barbara after learning that a year earlier, a fellow trooper had stopped mobster Carmine Galante in Apalachin, New York. After running a check on Galante, Croswell saw that he had a criminal record in New York City. Croswell later found that numerous local hotel rooms were being booked, and large quantities of food were being ordered for delivery to Barbara's home—he suspected something big was about to go down.

On November 14, 1957, over a hundred mobsters and bodyguards arrived at the property. Local law enforcement was on alert after seeing scores of expensive cars arriving at the residence.

The State Police set up roadblocks and raided the Barbara property with scores of federal, state, and local police. After realizing they were being raided, many mobsters drove off in a panic, only to be stopped at the roadblocks and placed under arrest. Other mobsters tried escaping on foot through the vast country woodlands, and some were successful. Over sixty men were apprehended, while fifty escaped, including Sam Cufari. Many top bosses were arrested, including Vito Genovese, Joseph Profaci, Joseph Bonanno, and Carlo Gambino. Twenty of the sixty men arrested were charged with Conspiracy to Obstruct Justice for lying about the intent of the organized criminal meeting. Most had stated they went to the estate for a barbeque and to wish Barbara well as he was recovering from an illness. The gangsters received fines of up to ten thousand dollars and were given sentences ranging from three to five years in prison. The following year all the convictions were overturned.

Until the Apalachin raid, the FBI, headed by J. Edgar Hoover, insisted there were no national organized criminal organizations in America. But the arrest of so many high-profile underworld characters prompted Hoover to begin investigating organized crime through surveillance, wiretaps, and the use of confidential informants.

In 1959, Vito Genovese was convicted of trafficking heroin and died in federal prison ten years later.

▼ ▼ ▼

One of the most serious rules in gangland organizations is never to have relations with another wiseguy's wife or girlfriend, especially if he's a Made guy. In 1972, Victor DeCaro made that mistake. DeCaro was known as a scrapper who liked to fight, and he was pretty good at it. The funny part is that he was a hairstylist by trade. Victor was also the son-in-law of Made member Skyball Scibelli, the right-hand enforcer of Sam Cufari. Years earlier, DeCaro had a run-in with three airmen at a bar in Agawam, and he ended up beating the three military guys to a pulp. Eventually, the airmen won a lawsuit against DeCaro's estate.

On May 23, 1972, Skyball picked up DeCaro to give him a ride to The Livingroom bar, where he was going to fill in for a sick bartender as a favor to his close friend, Amedeo Santaniello. That was the last time he was seen, until July 3, 1972, when his body was found in the Connecticut River wrapped in a tarp. He had been shot to death.

Sam had found out that DeCaro was fucking his wife, and DeCaro paid the ultimate price for his betrayal. Although law enforcement did an intensive investigation, no one was ever charged with the murder.

District Attorney Matthew Ryan had a reputation for being selective in prosecuting mobsters. Years before he was executed, Ryan had convicted DeCaro of the murder of Ralph Ramsdell after DeCaro pushed Ramsdell down a flight of stairs during an argument. DeCaro was sentenced to twelve years in state prison for manslaughter. It was widely known that Ryan didn't like DeCaro, and when he turned up dead, Ryan never bothered to open an investigation.

When a ballistics report was completed, it was determined that the same .38 caliber revolver used in DeCaro's murder was the same gun used in the shooting deaths of two other men. Gary Dube, a small-time criminal, was shot several times in the head and found in the Connecticut River wrapped in plastic and covered with lime. The other victim was Vincent Palmieri of New York. His body was found floating in a Vermont river, and had been riddled with bullets. Palmieri was the only one of the three who wasn't from the Springfield area.

Ultimately, Francis Soffen was arrested and pled guilty to the murder of Dube after a notorious bank robber, Stephen Perrot, testified against Soffen for the crime. There were never any suspects or arrests in the murders of both DeCaro and Palmieri.

Big Nose Sam Cufari died in 1983 of natural causes. He enjoyed being the boss of the Greater Springfield area, where he was known to play golf, eat at fine restaurants, and enjoy the company of beautiful women. Sam never saw the inside of a prison.

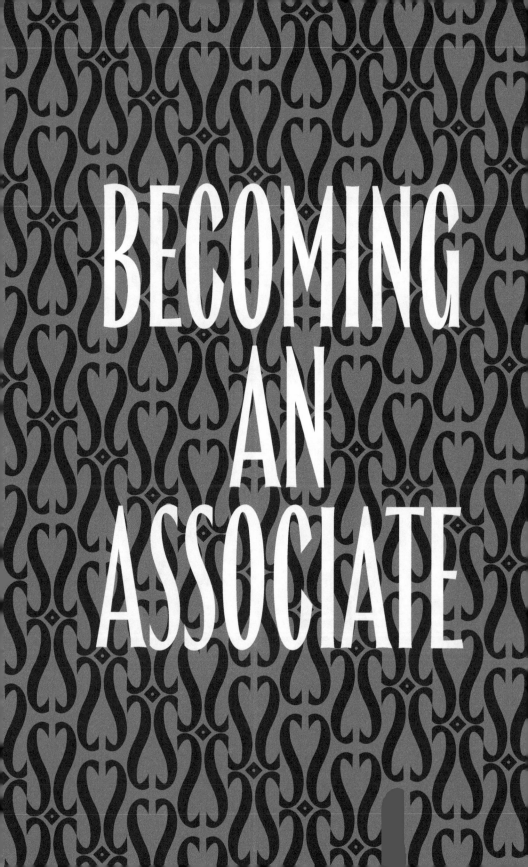

BECOMING AN ASSOCIATE

CHAPTER 5

When many people think of what it would be like to spend time in state prison, they would cringe with fear. They might imagine thoughts of being gang-raped by several hard-core lifers or getting shivved forty times with dull makeshift blades before being tossed off a thirty-foot tier.

But the reality is that if you have the right connections or are known to be affiliated with the Mafia, it can be a cakewalk. At least that's the way it was back in the early Nineties. And because of this I understand why many criminals continue to commit crimes after being released. To many of us, it's an easier life on the inside. As a convicted felon, finding a decent-paying job on the outside is nearly impossible once you have a felony conviction on your record. Today, most employers do background checks, and your resume gets tossed into the trash when they see that you're a convicted felon. When you're inside the prison walls, you have no responsibilities, and you aren't worried about where your next meal will come from.

In 1990 I was sentenced to a five-year sentence with a mandatory year in prison for carrying a handgun without a permit and firing a gun from a moving vehicle. When I first arrived, I was placed in a new-line cell with a guy doing life. This was only while I was being processed, and then I'd be moved to a more permanent cell. My cellmate was an ugly white guy with brown-stained teeth and greased-back black hair. He was several inches taller than me—I'm a little guy around five-seven, but I always keep in good shape. Immediately I didn't like him and thought he was a creep. His name was George, and he was pals with the guy housed in the next cell. They would chat back and forth, which would drive me crazy. And with a combined IQ of around fifty, the conversations were not very interesting. I lost many brains cells hearing their banter.

A few days after I arrived, I heard the guy in the next cell fucking his young cellmate, and it made my stomach turn. Afterward, I heard the kid weeping, which made me believe it wasn't a consensual act. The next day, George and his chickenhawk friend next door started with their incoherent chatter. That was when I found out my cellmate was also in on the anal action with the young guy in the next cell. He asked his pal when he would have another turn with the young guy. Right then, I wanted to kill them both.

The next day, I was moved out of my temporary cell and into my permanent cell with a regular guy who had pictures of his wife and kids hung on the walls. Still, I couldn't get the thought of those two lifers abusing that young kid to the point of him dropping tears.

It didn't take long for me to make friends on the inside. There aren't many secrets in prison, and everyone knows everybody else's business. They know who you are, why you're there, and who you're connected with. In many cases they even know if you're a family man and what you did for work before you were incarcerated. Information travels through many avenues of communication, including the screws, the other inmates in your prison, and inmates from other prisons who are in contact with cons at your facility. We had access to the media, and we were allowed regular phone calls where we got information on what was going on in the world. There were very few secrets on the inside.

A few weeks after I had arrived, my friend Bobby Giadoni and I gave some payback to the two guys raping the kid. We got the guy who was in the next cell after coming back from breakfast; we cornered him inside his cell like a rat.

"You like raping young guys," I said through clenched teeth.

I kicked him in the balls and when he buckled over, I punched him in the jaw, knocking him down.

"You fuckin' piece of shit. I could kill you!" I said.

We both continued kicking him in the groin and face until he was unconscious. His young roommate just stood watching with a smile growing with every blow. The guy that used to be my cellmate got the same, but not quite as badly as his lowlife friend. After they were beaten down, they were admitted to the infirmary. The guards had turned a blind eye to the beatings, and I'm sure they were happy to see the two predators carted off to the prison hospital.

▼ ▼ ▼

It was at Concord that I first met Ty Geas. That would be the start of a long, fruitful, and violent relationship.

There was a knock at my cell window.

"Yeah."

"Anthony?"

I remember looking into his eyes for the first time and they seemed vacant. "Yeah, what do you want?"

"My name is Ty Geas. My family told me to look you up. They are friends with the Euglianos."

"Is that right?" I knew that family and they were okay in my book.

"Yeah, I gotta go. I'm in J building, but I'll see you in the yard. Good meeting you."

"Alright, good meeting you," I said, and he was off.

A couple days later, we met in the yard, which was the start of our friendship. We worked out in the weight room and walked around the yard, doing laps at a fast pace to get the heartrate up. That's where he talked about his older brother Freddy. With a slight chuckle, he told me Freddy used to be a corrections officer at the York Street Jail in Springfield, and now, he was on the other side of the law.

In prison, cigarettes were like money, and wherever there was money to be made, I wanted in. I began a little loan-sharking business by giving inmates a couple of cartons of cigarettes with the understanding that when they got their commissary money they would give me back four cartons. Whatever the number of cartons I loaned out every day, I would get back double. I didn't smoke, and I would go on to sell some of my profits for cash.

I always had a knack for making money, and being in prison wasn't going to change that. I met a guy named Ronny inside, who was bragging about making tons of money selling coke on the outside, and saying that he still had an ongoing operation. Right away I knew I wanted to get in on the action, so I hooked him up with a friend of mine on the outside named Russell to set up a buy. I told him Russell had some quality powder and Ronny was excited to set up a deal. Ronny's people were going to buy a half-key from Russell in a parking lot of a restaurant just outside the Springfield city line. Ronny didn't know that I had set him up by having Russell sell Ronny's guy a half kilo of Inositol mixed with vitamin B. We made ten thousand on that scam. When Ronny told me about the rip-off, I played dumb and offered my sympathy.

I gave my friend two grand for perpetrating the con, and I walked away with the remaining eight thousand. Russell never existed—it was a fake name.

▼ ▼ ▼

After four months in Concord, I was transferred to do my remaining eight months at Gardner. This is where I met Freddy Geas for the first time. We met during a visiting session that was held outside, and Freddy was there to see his kid brother, Ty. Freddy would become my right-hand man, and we would ultimately commit murder together.

When you commit murder with someone, you forge a tight bond that will stay with you forever. Sometimes it can turn you against each other and might tempt you to try and kill each other.

Al Bruno was released from prison just before I got out. I was living at my parents' house in Springfield, relaxing in front of the television, when I heard a knock at the door. Bruno was standing on the front steps when I opened the door; he was just grinning at me.

"Hey, Al, come on in."

"How ya doing, kid?"

"I'm good, and you?"

"Fantastic." He smiled as I opened the door.

He followed me to the living room. "Have a seat."

"Anyone else home?" he asked as he scanned the inside of the house.

"No, just me. Can I get you a drink?"

"No, I'm good."

He sat in a chair, and I sat on the couch. He was wearing a dark blue sweatsuit with white stripes.

"So, what's up?" I had no idea why he came to the house. He had never come to the house before, and I was wondering if I did something wrong.

"How did your time go at Gardner?"

"It was okay. I met some interesting people and made a few bucks."

He smiled. "Yeah, I hear you're good at earning and you don't take shit from nobody."

"That's true, I don't." I was now thinking he came for a good reason.

"I came to ask if you want to work for me?" He hesitated with his eyes glued to mine. "To be part of my crew?"

I felt a bit of an adrenalin rush as I slowly started to comprehend what he was asking me. He was a Made guy with the Genovese family and he ran his own crew. This was what I had wanted since I was a kid—to be part of the Italian Mafia. It didn't take me long to respond.

"Yes, absolutely, yes!"

He opened a big smile. "Alright. Come and see me tomorrow, and we'll talk about how we can start making a lot of money together."

We both took to our feet, he opened his arms, and we embraced. "Thanks, Al. I appreciate it. I'll see you tomorrow."

"Tomorrow," he said as he turned toward the door.

I later found out that Anthony Delevo also wanted me to be part of his crew, and that he was going to approach me as well. Bruno beat him to the punch, and that caused some friction between them. I was glad I ended up in Bruno's crew because I never forgot about the day Delevo slapped me around in the back room of my father's store. The physical pain had subsided shortly afterwards, but the humiliation lingered. I still wanted to kill him for that.

It was around a week later that somebody told me to meet Bruno at my father's store, and when I arrived, Skyball was there. I had never had a real conversation with him—he was the boss of our area. Like me, Skyball wasn't a big guy. He was smaller than me, but he was known for being ruthless if you got on his wrong side.

"How's it going, kid?" Skyball asked.

"It's going good, Mr. Scibelli, thanks."

With Ralph Santaniello at my wedding, 1993

He smiled, and Bruno laughed. "Kid, you can call me Frank." He didn't like to be called Skyball.

"I asked Bingy to be part of my crew," Bruno said.

"I hear good things about you kid, and your father is a friend of mine." He moved in closer. "You want to be part of this life? Part of what we do."

"Yes, I do." I answered without hesitation.

He looked at Bruno. "Okay." He started to walk out, stopped, and turned around, and his eyes burned into mine. "You do what he tells you to do," he said pointing at Bruno. "If he tells you to jump, you ask, how high? You never talk to the cops or the feds. Am I clear?"

"Yes." I figured if I didn't do as he ordered, I could end up floating in the river.

"Alright. Get out there and earn us a lot of money."

He walked out, and Bruno followed. I stayed behind, feeling like I had grown an inch or two taller.

I knew if I was going to move up the ladder and eventually become a Made guy, I had to produce. So I began by getting the word out to all the degenerate gamblers that booked games with me and my friends, and I set up a floating casino. This is a casino that was always moving from place to place to avoid getting raided. We would get the word out in the underground on where and when the next casino would be in operation.

I bought some used tables, and we were in business. We had blackjack and craps games held at Italian social clubs and in the backrooms of bars owned by wiseguys. One of our best venues was at Gabby's bar in Westfield, which I owned with Freddy. It didn't take long before we took in around ten to twenty thousand a night. The deal I had with Bruno was a fifty-fifty split, and he was very happy with what I had accomplished in such a short period of time.

Another means of earning was by loan-sharking. Again, I was doing it with Bruno, but I also had my own thing going on the side with my friend Albert. He was a local guy who would loan me cash with a 2 percent vig fee. In turn, I would lend some money on a 5 percent vig, profiting 3 percent on the loans. Although this was profitable, it was also risky going behind Bruno's back.

On occasion, someone wouldn't pay us in time. As the interest piled up week after week, it became harder for people to come up with the entire amount, so they paid their weekly interest in many cases. The ones who failed to pay had to be persuaded to pay up through threats of violence; and if that didn't work, they would collect a beating. One that comes to mind was a guy that owed me forty-five grand, stopped paying, and went into hiding. I caught up to him a few weeks later as he came out of a bar. Me, Ralphie Santaniello, and Louie Santos severely beat him with baseball bats to the point he was admitted to the hospital. Three days later, we were paid in full.

Selling large quantities of cocaine was very lucrative for us. Working with different partners, we bought kilos on a weekly basis from a guy in South Boston affiliated with Whitey Bulger's Winter Hill Gang. A key would cost us twenty-two thousand, and it was close to being pure coke, making it possible to cut it a hundred percent. We would break it up into quarter-keys and resell it. The profit was a hundred percent—earning us around twenty thousand a week. Bruno wasn't part of any of the drug deals I had going on. He made it clear that if I dealt drugs, he would kill me. That made it a very risky business.

The bookmaking business began to flourish, grossing me around four-hundred thousand a week, with a net profit of about a hundred-and-fifty thousand, which I had to split with Bruno. The cash was rolling in, but there was one problem: I was a degenerate gambler. Sometimes I bet up to a hundred thousand a day.

Working with a couple of other guys, we were buying and selling a hundred-and-fifty pounds of marijuana a week and netting around sixty thousand dollars. At one point, we had a half million in our kitty, which I usually kept hidden at my parent's house. We used that money to buy drugs, and we would split the profits as the amount in the kitty grew too large.

With everything I had going on, I was busy from the moment I woke up until I hit the pillow. But at the end of the day, I would normally go out to have a great dinner with the guys or my girlfriend. We ate at the finest restaurants, ordered the best steaks and seafood, drank five-hundred-dollar bottles of wine, high-end cognac, and scotch. We sometimes ordered Louis the Thirteenth Cognac at a price of a hundred-and-fifty a shot. I was on top of the world.

Hijacking trucks was another means of earning money, which we would do around once a month. We would hijack the trucks in three different ways. Either we would hitch a parked trailer to our tractor and drive away with the load, or we would break in and unload all the contents into another truck and drive away. We occasionally robbed trucks at gunpoint, but that was risky, so it was normally the last resort. We usually targeted trucks where we had an inside guy who worked for the company, and we would know which trucks to hit and if there were any security risks. Typically, we would go after loads of large-screen televisions, appliances, and cigarettes. Then we would drive the goods to Boston, where we would sell the contents for around a hundred thousand dollars.

There is one robbery that comes to mind. I knew a couple of guys from Albany who I had done some pot deals with in the past. They told me they had stolen a trailer and wanted to sell the contents that consisted of flat-screen TVs and appliances. I told them I knew a couple of interested guys, and I set up a meeting in a secluded area of Springfield.

The night of the robbery, I was with Freddy, Ralph, Sammy, and Louie and we were all packed into one car.

"Pull over here," I said to Freddy, who was driving. I was in the back with Sammy and Ralph, and Louie was riding shotgun.

"These motherfuckers better be on time," Louie said. "I'm not feeling too comfortable sitting here with loaded guns."

"They'll be here," I said. "They trust me."

"Well, that's their first mistake," Sammy said with a twisted smirk.

"Yeah, that's like trusting a wolf to watch your fucking chickens," Freddy said, and we all started laughing.

"What!? I'm not trustworthy?" I said. "Look at me. This face should be on a stamp."

"Well, if it was, you wouldn't have to worry about anyone stealing those fucking worthless stamps," Ralph said, and we laughed again.

Freddy saw headlights appear in his rearview mirror. "I think they're here," he said as he pulled a ski hat over his face.

"Put your mask on," I said to Louie, and I nudged Sammy to do the same. "Get ready!"

The truck pulled up behind us and stopped. "Get the guns ready," I said.

Freddy, Louie, and Sammy were out of the car within seconds. They surrounded the truck with their guns drawn.

"Get the fuck out of the truck!" Sammy yelled.

The two guys in the cab sat motionless as they realized what was happening. They were double-crossed and were being robbed at gunpoint.

Freddy climbed up to the passenger side with his pistol and placed the barrel against the window. "Get the fuck out of the truck, or I'll shoot you in the fucking face!" He said in a soft, firm tone.

The two guys opened the doors and got out.

"Where's Anthony?" the taller guy asked.

"We don't know any, Anthony," Louie said. "Now, start running," he pointed his gun at one and then the other.

The two very shaken guys began walking away.

"I said run!" Louie barked, and he followed with a gunshot, disturbing the night air. They started sprinting. "Run, Forest Run," Louie said as he shot at them while they darted through the field.

"What the fuck, Louie," I said. "Why are you shooting at them?"

"They were moving too slowly, so I thought I'd motivate them."

"Right, and you probably motivated the cops too. Did you get the keys?"

Sammy held up the keys. "I got 'em."

"Alright, you know the plan. Let's get the hell out of here before the cops get here." I took one more look at Louie, and he knew I wasn't happy.

We sold the load in Boston, made a hundred and twenty grand, and split it five ways.

Soon after the robbery, I decided it was time to break away from my partners in the pot and coke business and go off on my own. Some guys were partying too hard and snorting away some of our profits. I didn't do drugs and figured I would make a lot more money on my own—I was right.

In 1997 I had $1.3 million in cash at the house. Mostly in increments of twenty, fifty, and hundred-dollar bills. I had borrowed a hundred grand from my father to get started in my solo drug-dealing business, and my family and I were now living very comfortably. My wife Irene didn't ask many questions about how I made my money, and I never brought the subject up—we didn't talk about it.

"We made it, baby," I said as we sat in the kitchen.

"Yes, we did." She handed me a bottle of Dom Perignon, and I popped it open and poured.

"Salut," I said, raising my glass, and we toasted to the good life.

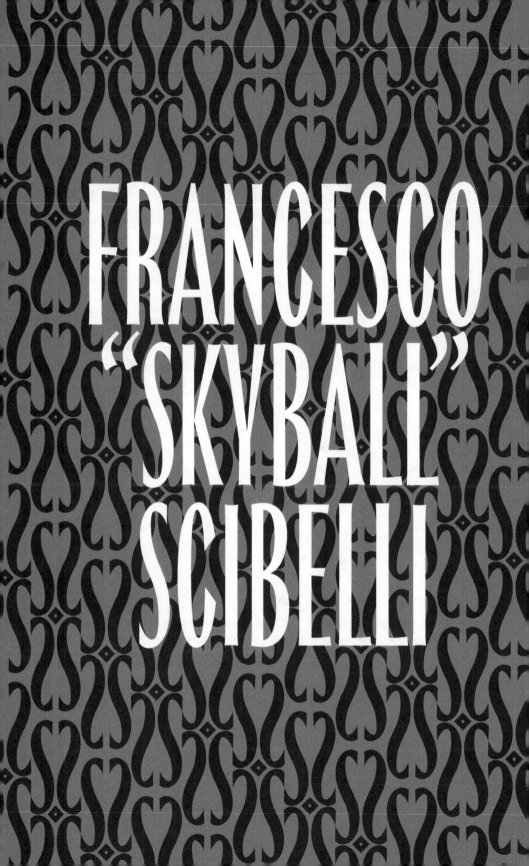

FRANCESCO "SKYBALL" SCIBELLI

CHAPTER 6

After the retirement of Big Nose Sam in 1980, his natural successor was "Skyball" Scibelli, who had been his strongman for many decades. Skyball was born in Springfield in September of 1912. His parents, who migrated from Italy, also had two other sons, Albert and Anthony, both younger than Skyball. Albert "Baba" Scibelli was also a major player in the organization and would enjoy a short reign as captain after the demotion of Skyball. His brother Anthony "Turk" Scibelli was an associate who helped run numbers, but he was not nearly as significant as his older brothers. Unlike Cufari, Skyball would spend his life in and out of prison for various crimes, including illegal gambling, extortion, racketeering, bookmaking, and assault and battery. Also unlike Cufari, Skyball was known to have a violent and explosive temper and was widely feared for a guy who probably weighed less than a hundred and sixty pounds.

For reasons unknown, Skyball hated Joe Alamo—possibly because Alamo was a drug dealer or because he had crossed Skyball at one time or another. In broad daylight, Skyball pistol-whipped him in front of Ciro's Restaurant on Main Steet, causing him to seek serious medical attention.

In another instance, Skyball was angry that he wasn't invited to Bruno's coming-home party after he was released from prison. Amedeo Santaniello was the event planner and when Skyball saw him at La Fiorentina Pastry Shop, he had Anthony Delevo, Felix Tranghese, and Jake Nettis drag him

Skyball
Scibelli

into the men's room and shoved his head in the toilet and flushed. He was the capo of the Springfield Crew and felt slighted that he was overlooked.

▼ ▼ ▼

Skyball began his criminal career in the 1930s by committing extortion, illegal gambling, and selling liquor on Sundays. For these crimes, he was arrested in 1932 and sentenced to prison. After his release, he continued his criminal activities working under Cufari as part of the Genovese family. It is unclear when Skyball was inducted into the family to become a Made guy, but it most likely occurred in the early 1950s. Unlike modern times, back then wiseguys knew how to keep things quiet, and they would take secrets to the grave.

As time went on, in a forever-changing world, it became much more difficult to avoid the long arm of the law. The federal agencies were now empowered with modern technological devices for surveillance and wire-tapping. In addition, in 1970, the RICO Law was enacted, giving agents and prosecutors much more power in enforcing and prosecuting crimi-nal organizations. In the past, they could only go after individuals, but by enacting the "Racketeering Influenced and Corrupt Organizations" law enforcement officers could link groups of criminals together and charge them. RICO was also a decisive blow to mobsters because it carried prison terms of up to twenty years.

In 1961, Skyball was arrested along with sidekick Paul "The Penman" Cardaropoli for running a gambling ring out of phone booths at Our Lady of Providence Hospital in Holyoke, Massachusetts. Both men had a rep-utation for their shrewd abilities in handicapping horse racing and they were considered gaming experts. A Catholic nun who observed the criminal activity informed the police. As a result, they were arrested at the hospital on a bookmaking charge and sentenced to nineteen months in prison.

Serving as Cufari's enforcers, Skyball and his cousin, Felix Tranghese, were his primary sources of muscle. The two cousins' parents came from Quindici, Italy, a small village near Naples, and this along with both being Made soldiers gave them a strong bond. The pair of cousins were both

inducted into the Genovese family as Made members and were now soldiers. These wiseguys had a reputation for committing acts of violence
to maintain the organizational integrity of the family. Their weapon of
choice was often baseball bats. Cufari was smart because he kept his distance from criminal activities and violence by delegating to Skyball, using
him as a buffer.

Victor DeCaro, whose bullet-riddled body was pulled from the
Connecticut River in 1979, was Skyball's son-in-law. Although Skyball was
the last person seen with DeCaro and was a suspect in his murder, no charges
were ever brought against him. Remember: DeCaro made the mistake of
fucking Cufari's wife.

Another shooting Skyball was tied to but never charged with was the attack
on Joseph Maruca in 1981 in Agawam, Massachusetts. Maruca was a gangster linked to the Bufalino family out of Binghamton, New York. He had
traveled to Springfield on several occasions to meet with Michael DeMarco,
whose real name was Jake Nettis. Jake was a lifelong gangster with ties to
the Genovese family, but he was never inducted into the family.

As Bruno, Delevo, and Campiti hid waiting in a barn for Joseph Maruca
to show up, they intended to kill him. The barn in Agawam, Massachusetts, was owned by his brother, Frank Bruno, and housed cases of canned
tomatoes. Maruca thought he was collecting a debt paid in tomatoes for
his family in upstate New York, when in fact, they set him up to be killed
for stealing money from their gambling operation. After entering the barn,
Bruno fired his gun but only managed to shoot off Maruca's ear. Maruca
then took four additional bullets from his assailants. After being shot five
times, he managed to run away from the barn and escape into the neighborhood. Bruno and Castagna returned to the restaurant and handed the
guns to Skyball for disposal. Afterward they all agreed Bruno needed many
hours of shooting practice—they all did. Some labeled them "The gang who
couldn't shoot straight." Maruca survived the attack but refused to talk.
Later, another government witness, hitman Phil Leonetti, testified about
the attempted murder, and Bruno and Jake Nettis were charged. Bruno was
eventually acquitted and Nettis was sentenced to ten years in prison and
released after three.

One of the many mistakes made by wiseguys is using small-caliber weapons on hits, such as .22 caliber handguns. Also, instead of surprising the target and shooting them at point blank, they fire from a distance, allowing the victim to escape. Successful hitmen would normally use a .38 caliber weapon at the very least, and they would pull the trigger while standing inches away. Bruno and Nettis fired from a distance. Bruno was charged and acquitted; Nettis was sentenced to ten years in prison and released after three.

▼ ▼ ▼

Skyball and his brother, Albert "Baba" Scibelli, had been operating a very successful vending-machine company. They had machines in nearly every bar in the city of Springfield and surrounding towns. The poker machines would pay off in cash from the bartender, and they also had cigarette and snack machines and video games. This was a huge source of income for the family. However, it was causing a lot of friction with the Patriarca family out of Providence, who wanted a piece of the business.

The Scibelli brothers were adamantly against the idea, but the Patriarcas went behind their backs and began placing their machines in bars already occupied with Scibelli's machines. It started to get ugly as Scibelli's guys were smashing Patriarca's machines and pushing them into the street. In addition, bartenders were getting beat up for allowing the rivals to bring in their machines. Finally, the opposing families scheduled a sit-down meeting in Worcester, Massachusetts. Carlo Mastrototaro, the guy running Worcester, chaired the meeting. They came to an agreement that the Scibellis would maintain control over the city of Springfield, and they would share the surrounding towns with the Patriarcas.

During the warm season, Skyball would spend much of his time in Old Saybrook, Connecticut, where he owned two houses. Even though it was an hour's drive from Springfield, he continued his criminal activities by overseeing an illegal gambling operation out of the Terra Mar Yacht and Tennis Club.

While on probation in 1986, Skyball and his friend, Anthony Volpe, severely beat a man at the Side Porch Restaurant in Old Saybrook. After the man refused to get off the phone, Volpe beat him down, causing severe lacerations and blunt-force trauma to his face and body. He had to be taken to the hospital for treatment.

As in many cases, wiseguys are two completely different people at home and on the street. For example, mobster Roy DeMeo of the Gambino family in New York is believed to have murdered over two hundred people. Not only did he kill them, but he also cut their bodies into six pieces with a hacksaw and knife. Yet, to this day, his wife and children say he was a loving, kind, and gentle husband and father.

Skyball's neighbors in Old Saybrook described him as a quiet gentleman who used to take walks around the neighborhood, often stopping for brief conversations with people in the community. He was also known for routinely swimming in Long Island Sound. Many of his neighbors knew his reputation, but they didn't see that side of him. Instead, they knew him as a family man.

▼ ▼ ▼

Some may wonder how Skyball escaped justice to live a comfortable life along the Connecticut shore for most of his golden years. The simple truth is that he was friendly with corrupt District Attorney Matthew Ryan. It is widely known that they spent time together at bars and restaurants, enjoying shared power on both spectrums.

Ryan was alleged to have practiced "The Springfield Special," where he was selective in whom he prosecuted and for what crimes. Many people would ask, when the chief law enforcement officer in the city is unethical and probably committing crimes, how can we expect our citizens to be lawful?

Skyball Scibelli retired in 1998, soon after his release from prison, and in 2000 he died of natural causes.

PASSING
THE TORCH

CHAPTER 7

Al Bruno had a reputation for bad-mouthing other wiseguys, especially when attempting to advance himself among the ranks. Bruno enjoyed bending the ear of Frank "Farby" Serpico, his primary contact with the New York faction of the Genovese family. He often told tales of how Skyball was getting old and going senile. Bruno was planting a seed on how Skyball was forgetful and unable to earn and run the Springfield Crew as he had in the past. After a while, it sunk in, and in 1996, Skyball got demoted back to soldier status. Bruno was now grinning ear to ear, thinking his time had arrived and he would become boss of the Springfield area. His grin soon turned to a frown, however, when New York decided to make Skyball's younger brother Baba the capo of Springfield.

Albert "Baba" Scibelli was born in 1920, eight years after his brother Skyball took his first breath. Born in Springfield, Baba lived most of his life in the South-End—called "Little Italy" by most locals. Baba joined the Navy and served during the Second World War, and when he was discharged, he began his life as a gangster. Baba was a quiet and reserved character, unlike his older brother, and he was thought to have become a millionaire by the time he turned thirty-five. With an inherent ability to make money, Baba grew his fortune into the tens of millions throughout his tenure as a mobster.

Baba was a family man who enjoyed the finer things in life. He was a flashy and good-looking guy who always drove fancy cars and wore expensive suits and jewelry. As he walked down the street, he was the kind of guy that people wondered who he was and where he was going.

Even though Baba made money in many different areas, most of his fortune came from vending machines, both legal and illegal. He was also a silent owner of several legitimate businesses, including bars and restaurants. During the four years Baba was running the Springfield Crew, things were calmer than they had been in the past, and everyone in his crew was making good money. He was adamant about maintaining a low profile with law enforcement and he insisted that his crew avoid violent confrontations.

In 1996, Baba proposed that Emilio Fusco become a Made member of the Genovese family, and he was inducted shortly after that. But Fusco was known to be a talker, and that was ultimately his undoing. After being caught incriminating himself and other wiseguys on a wiretap, the indictments soon followed. After a fifteen-month investigation, law enforcement finally moved in to arrest nine mobsters in December of 2000, which was the biggest sting in Springfield Mob history.

After the arrests, the keys were turned over to Anthony Delevo, who was being groomed to assume the role of captain of the family. The New York bosses ended up shelving Baba after he admitted to the authorities that he was a Made member of the Genovese family. This was of course a huge violation of the family rules.

Anthony Delevo was a hothead who would fly off the handle without notice and was well-known for committing acts of violence. Delevo wasn't a guy who drove nice cars and wore expensive clothes. He kept a low profile and lived as an average middle-class guy—but he was a multimillionaire.

In 1980, he was stopped in Connecticut with two other guys, and in the car they found two handguns and two shotguns, along with a pile of betting slips and they were all arrested. After a plea bargain, Delevo only received a suspended sentence and a fine. Five years later, he was arrested during a raid in the back room of a strip club while involved in an illegal blackjack game; and four years after that, he was arrested for running an illegal gambling business. In 1991, Delevo was an unindicted co-conspirator in the

Baba Scibelli

attempted murder of Joseph Maruca. Finally, in 2003, Delevo pled guilty and was sentenced to prison along with several other mobsters indicted in the raid that occurred in 2000.

Baba was never sent to prison and lived to the age of ninety-one, ultimately dying of natural causes. Delevo died in prison in 2005 of cancer. He was sixty-five years old.

CHAPTER 8

Adolfo Bruno was born in, Bracigliano, Italy, on November 24, 1945, and he immigrated to New York City ten years later, eventually making his way to Springfield. As Bruno worked his way up the ranks of the Genovese family, it is unknown exactly when he became a Made member. In 1976, his long-time friend, Amadeo Santaniello, also from Bracigliano, migrated to Springfield to join Bruno as his right-hand man. The two wiseguys would partner together on many business ventures until they had a falling out in later years. Bruno, who started as a soldier under Sam Cufari, became one of Skyball Scibelli's biggest earners after Skyball took over when Cufari retired.

Although Bruno had never properly learned to read and write, he was street-smart and knew how to make money for the family. He was cautious and kept a low profile until his arrest in 1979 for illegal gambling and conspiracy charges. In March of that same year, the body of feared mob associate Antonio Facente was found in the trunk of his car. He had been tortured and shot six times, and he had diapers wrapped around his head. Bruno had bragged to me that using diapers was a good way to keep blood from pooling.

Facente was a street fighter, and he had a reputation as a loose cannon who wasn't afraid of anyone. In 1972, Facente was convicted of the murder

Big Al Bruno

of a Springfield business owner who he shot over unpaid loans. That conviction was eventually overturned, partly because of racial slurs directed at him by District Attorney Ryan. It was no secret that Ryan hated Facente, and when his daughter began having an affair with him, Ryan was livid and determined to end the affair.

Bruno was a bit surprised when Ryan approached him, asking for a favor. The pair had been seen on many occasions playing racquetball together, and they had a friendly relationship. Ryan told Bruno that Facente was seeing his daughter and that he had gotten her hooked on drugs, and he asked Bruno to take care of him. Bruno later told me that was music to his ears because he figured this was a good way to get the DA in his pocket. Bruno said he wasn't sure if Ryan just wanted him to break a leg or simply scare him, but he knew what he had to do to control future Mob court cases.

Skyball, who was the boss at the time, knew Bruno was very friendly with the DA, and when Ryan approached Bruno, they had put a plan in place. They figured if it worked, they would be able to keep their crew protected from the law while watching their rivals fall into the justice system. I personally benefited from the protection of the corrupt district attorney by avoiding cases brought against me and having charges dropped over several years.

Bruno was never charged in the murder, and statements linking him to the Facente murder were hidden from the public record and buried somewhere in the bowels of the Hampden Superior Courthouse.

After serving as District Attorney for thirty-two years, Ryan retired in 1990. Although Ryan had a reputation as a solid, no-nonsense prosecutor, who had won many high-profile murder cases, his legacy would be stained in the end. Allegations of fixing Mob-related cases and covering up the murder of altar boy Daniel Croteau would haunt him. Croteau a thirteen-year-old boy was found bludgeoned to death in Chicopee, and the only suspect in the murder was Catholic Priest Richard Lavigne.

Ryan was known to have a close relationship with Bishop Weldon, who feared backlash if one of his priests was brought up on murder charges.

In addition, evidence and witness testimony had mysteriously disappeared from the case file. As for suspects, there were never any other than Lavigne, who was later defrocked for molesting over fifty children.

In 2021, Springfield District Attorney Anthony Gulluni announced they were going to arrest Lavigne in the cold case; however, justice would never be served because Lavigne died on the same day the indictment was issued. He was eighty years old.

Matthew Ryan died of natural causes in 2009.

▼ ▼ ▼

Al Bruno was known as a larger-than-life character who was often seen wearing Hawaiian shirts, large-rimmed glasses, and sometimes smoking oversized cigars. Bruno earned a lot of money and spent it as fast as he made it. He was a generous guy when it came to people who were not in the game, and he often put the squeeze on the guys in his crew in order to fill his own pockets. If one of his wiseguys made a buck, he demanded 50 percent of the take, even though he had nothing to do with the caper. This caused a lot of friction amongst his crew and prompted many of them to go behind his back, make deals, and commit crimes without his knowledge.

Bruno had a hand in most illegal activities, including loan-sharking, extortion, gambling, numbers, robberies, and Vegas gambling junkets. But he was old-school when it came to narcotics. He was adamantly against any of his guys getting involved in selling drugs. Bruno figured drugs brought a lot of heat from law enforcement, and he didn't trust that people would keep their mouths shut after being arrested for crimes that brought very long prison sentences. As a result, he often threatened guys in his crew, stating he would kill them if he found out they were selling drugs.

When it came to pulling people together, Bruno was a master. He would drive to New York, Boston, Providence, Connecticut, New Jersey, Philadelphia, Albany, and Upstate New York to meet with other mobsters.

He would create bonds that often cemented deals with other regions, and everyone involved would make a lot of money.

▼ ▼ ▼

Vito Ricciardi was a barber whose shop was in East Springfield; a stone's throw away from my grandmother's house where I lived for several years. He was a friendly little guy from the old country, and he spoke with a heavy accent. Vito was friends with Gaetano Milano, a Made guy in the Patriarca crime family. Milano was doing time for the murder of Billy Grasso, and he asked Vito to help him by collecting loan-sharking debts on the street that were owed to him. When Vito went to collect, the guys who owed Milano said they had already made the payments to Al Bruno. Unknown to Milano, Bruno was approaching his customers and telling them he was assuming the debts. When Vito told Milano what happened, he was furious and asked Vito to confront Bruno for his treachery.

In 1993, Vito went to the Italian social club, Our Lady of Mount Carmel, where Bruno was known to hang out and play cards. He asked Bruno why he was moving in on Milano's operation, and Bruno began slapping him around. In a rage, Vito pulled out a handgun and began shooting at Bruno, who immediately ducked, taking cover. Vito fled the club, and Bruno was unharmed. Vito is believed to have shot high, purposely not trying to hit Bruno, but only to scare him.

With revenge gnawing at his core, Bruno made it clear to his crew that he would kill Vito for daring to shoot at him. He was a Made guy, and this couldn't go unpunished. After careful consideration, he decided to have Vito killed when he traveled to Italy. Bruno contacted Biaggio Cava, a Mafia boss in Italy, and asked him to take care of Vito on his next trip out, and he agreed. It never happened.

▼ ▼ ▼

Bruno owned many bars and restaurants in the Greater Springfield area, but Cara Mia was his principal business place. It was located on East Columbus

Avenue in Springfield and was considered one of the best Italian restaurants in the city. This was a place Bruno would meet with people to eat, drink, and close deals, and it was managed by his closest friend, Amedeo Santaniello.

In the winter of 2001, a small gathering of wiseguys sat drinking, eating, and sharing stories of the past. The boss from New York, Artie Nigro, had driven up for dinner along with Pasquale DeLuca. Bruno had some of his guys in attendance, including me, Felix Tranghese, and Joey Basile. This was the night Bruno was told he was being promoted to captain of the Western New England faction of the Genovese family. He would oversee Springfield, Hartford, and Albany, and New Haven was to be shared with the Patriarca family.

Bruno was in his glory, and he was smiling ear-to-ear. Artie stood and offered a toast, making it clear that Bruno was now the area's boss and they had to obey him. That night Bruno drank his fill with his chin raised a notch higher than usual. Over the past few years, Bruno had been drinking a lot more than he used to, and he was getting sloppy. Artie had noticed but gave him the benefit of the doubt. It was frowned upon for Made guys to get hammered on a regular basis, and it was risky to have a boss who wasn't in control of his faculties while running the business. This, along with his relentless greed and cooperation with the FBI, ultimately led to his demise.

MY
SPRINGFIELD
CREW

CHAPTER 9

During my life as a gangster, I partnered and worked with many people, including Anthony Scibelli, Reno Ceravolo, Frankie Depergola, John Calabrese, Richie Valentini, Dave Cecchetelli, and Steve Marshall. But the main guys who worked with me throughout the years are covered in this chapter.

▼ ▼ ▼

Fotios "Freddy" Geas: When it came down to it, Freddy was the closest crew member to me. There were guys I grew up with and knew most of my life, and we were tight, but my relationship with Freddy was different. The bond between people who commit murder together is an intimate kind of connection. Taking a person's life is an act that will stay with you forever. When you share that with another person, only the people involved can truly understand the depth and darkness of watching another person draw their last breath by your hand. A bond is formed through a shared secret that cannot be compromised by disclosing the murder to anyone. If that secret bond is broken by one person by revealing the murder to another, that person has committed an act of betrayal. And if this deadly secret is disclosed, one person may begin plotting to kill the other for violating the trust. In our life, the suspicion that someone might talk can cause many gangsters to kill each other without actual proof of their actions. I also shared a bond with

Freddy's younger brother, Ty, but it was different from the one I had with Freddy, as I will reveal later.

Freddy was a guy I knew I could trust. He was a carefree kind of guy, laid back, yet he had a keen outlook on the world around him. Freddy wasn't a big drinker and never touched drugs. He wasn't flashy; he was just a good-looking, clean-cut guy. Freddy was typically dressed down in jeans and a nice shirt. If you saw him on the street, you might think he was a salesman or an insurance underwriter. He had a good sense of humor, and we shared many laughs, continuously busting each other's balls over the years. Although Freddy was low-key, he was prone to violence when necessary. He was the kind of guy who wasn't afraid of anyone, and if he didn't think he could win with his hands, he would use a bat, knife, or gun to prevail. That's the way it was with many of my friends. If we knew a guy was a martial arts expert or a professional boxer, we wouldn't try to fight him with fists; we would use a weapon.

Many people don't know this, but in the late 1980s, Freddy was a corrections officer at the York Street Jail in Springfield. His tenure was short-lived, however, after he beat the shit out of his boss and was fired. After that, he worked at his uncle's jewelry store, selling watches, chains, necklaces, earrings, and rings. Freddy always wore nice watches; later in his life, he sported Rolexes.

Out of all the gangsters I have known over the years, I would rank Freddy at the top of my list regarding grifting. He was a cunning con artist, very gifted at convincing his mark that he was trustworthy. Ultimately they would learn differently, but it would be too late. Some of his best scams were selling fake bricks of coke, and he would make off with thousands of dollars. Freddy was also in the stolen-credit-card racket. He would get card numbers and steal the mark's identity long enough to go on shopping sprees. In turn, he would sell the items on the street. Freddy was an adept jeweler who learned a lot working at his uncle's jewelry store, and later in life he was selling fake Rolexes on the street. These were high-end fakes, where the second hand moved smoothly around the face. To say that they were knock-offs someone would have had to take the watch apart and be familiar with the internal mechanism.

Being a good father was important to Freddy, and he always made sure he spent time with his two kids. Even though his marriage only lasted a few years, he remained present in his kids' life after the divorce was finalized. He has a daughter and a son, and I'm told he stays in contact with them from prison.

After he was released from prison in 2001, I noticed a change in Freddy. He had been inside for four years, and that amount of time could change a person. He seemed much bolder and carried a sense of entitlement because he was now a convict. He looked at other hustlers on the street differently if they hadn't done hard time. In his eyes, they hadn't yet earned their bones because they never shared a cell with hardened criminals and killers. Freddy *now* had the eye of the tiger. As time went on, and he began killing people, I noticed he started to develop a taste for it. It gave him a sense of power. Freddy wanted to be remembered as a killer to be revered by some and feared by many. He would go on to be charged with killing Whitey Bulger.

▼ ▼ ▼

Tyler "Ty" Geas: Out of all the guys I have known in the game, Ty was the most dangerous. I had to pay close attention to him. It wasn't because he was the toughest guy I had ever met; it was because he was paranoid and an extremely violent killer. Although we were friendly, I knew if it came down to it, he would try and kill me, and I would have to kill him first. If I killed one of the Geas brothers, I'd have to kill them both, which wouldn't be an easy task. Ty was good with his hands and had no fear. But he was always worried that someone was out to get him, which made him dangerous. He was an accomplished high school wrestler, and he was built like a Greek God. Ty wasn't as tall as Freddy and he was several pounds lighter, but he was strong and fast. He liked the ladies and spent a lot of time with strippers; he liked the hard-body type. Ty wasn't a heavy drinker, and like his brother Freddy, he never touched drugs.

Unlike his brother Freddy, Ty had a temper and could become unhinged in a split second. He was good with his fists but preferred to use weapons, and he often carried a gun. I had also seen him carry, and sometimes use, a crossbow, icepick, knife, bat, and a blackjack. I didn't know Ty as well as Freddy because he wasn't on the street as often. Ty had spent the better part of his life behind bars and much of that time in solitary confinement for beating up corrections officers or other inmates. On the street, he had a reputation as someone to avoid, but he was a major part of my crew, and I could count on him to get things done without hesitation. For example, Ty was involved in helping me move significant quantities of marijuana and was good at it—he was a hustler.

A bunch of us were at the Mardi Gras, a strip club in Springfield, and we were having drinks in a private area of the place. Everyone was having a good time, but there was one guy with us who tended to drink way too much. He was a good guy, but when he got drunk, he was sloppy and provocative. The guy was a successful bookmaker who was moving hundreds of thousands of dollars in cash on sports betting. After too many drinks, he approached Ty and began taunting him by hanging on him and pretending to get him in a headlock. Although he was kidding around, it quickly got out of control and Ty hit him with one quick elbow to the face and knocked him out cold.

After he came around, we got the bookmaker out of the bar, and I saw to it that he eventually got home safely. A few days later, I had to clear the air with his brother, a respectable guy who was known to carry a gun and wouldn't be afraid to use it to protect his family. After telling him what happened, he understood and didn't have any hard feelings, and that was the end of it.

Detective John "Blondie" Delaney was a fair but no-nonsense narcotics officer. He was outside of the Hippodrome nightclub when he observed a commotion. Ty was beating the shit out of the owner Steve Stein and Delaney arrested him while his brother Freddy stood nearby watching. Delaney went on to say that Ty knew he was there and was watching him when he attacked Stein. He added that people who have no fear of being locked up are a real danger to the public.

These are just a couple of the many times Ty had gotten into beefs with people, but the run-in with Bruno was the one where I may have helped save his life.

Freddy was getting fake Rolex watches from a guy in South Boston. These fakes were so real looking that you couldn't tell unless you were a watchmaker.

Freddy Geas

He was buying them for two grand and selling them for four. Freddy approached Bruno's son Victor and said he would sell him a watch for thirty-five hundred. Victor said he wanted a professional jeweler to look at it first to make sure it was real. Freddy agreed and gave him the watch—no cash was exchanged.

The next time he saw Victor, he told Freddy that the watch was a fake, so Freddy asked for him to give it back. Victor went on to say he didn't have it because it was stolen from his car by a valet attendant. At that time, Freddy was just out of prison and was short on cash, and he owed the guy from Boston two thousand. After negotiating, Victor agreed to give Freddy the two grand so he could cover his cost. Soon after, Victor told his father that Freddy had sold him a fake Rolex and that he thought I was involved in the scam.

I was sitting in my car outside the Italian club, and Ty was in his car parked next to mine. Our driver-side windows faced each other, and we were talking when Bruno beeped me, so I called him.

"Hello."

"Where the fuck are you?"

"I'm at the club," I said.

"No, you're not. I'm at the club."

"I'm outside in the parking lot."

"Wait there. I'm coming out."

I could tell by his tone that he was pissed about something. We watched him come out, and he approached us, standing in between our cars.

"What's this? I hear you and that scumbag Freddy sold my son a fake Rolex?"

"Al, first of all, I had nothing to do with that. Second, Freddy gave Victor a watch to have checked out, and he didn't take any money from him."

"Bullshit! Victor paid him two thousand."

"Yeah, that was after the fact."

"Was the watch a fake?"

"Yes."

"That scumbag is selling fake watches to my family. I'm gonna give that scumbag a serious headache."

"My brother isn't a scumbag," Ty said.

"Yes, he is. He's a fucking scumbag." Bruno yelled while staring Ty down.

"Don't call my brother a scumbag," Ty said in an elevated tone.

At that very second, Al backhanded Ty across the face.

"I said he's a fucking scumbag, you fucking scumbag!"

Al slapped him two more times. "I'll deal with your brother later. Now, you two get the fuck outta here." Al stormed back into the club.

"I'm gonna kill that motherfucker!" Ty said.

I was pretty sure if Ty had his gun on him, he would have.

"Come on. I'll meet you at the Civic Pub, and we can talk."

"Okay." Ty said as he shifted his car into gear.

We sat at a table at the pub in front of a couple of drinks. I could see the embarrassed look on Ty's face. Nobody had ever put their hands on him like that and walked away unscathed, not even corrections officers.

"I'm gonna waste that prick."

"Ty, he was out of line, but you got to let it go."

"Fuck that. Nobody slaps me around. And nobody calls my brother a scumbag."

"Listen, it was just a slap," I said. "It's not like he beat up your mother. If you kill him, where does that leave you? If you don't get grabbed on a murder rap by the cops, which you probably will, Al is a Made guy. You know the price for killing a Made guy." I grabbed his arm to get his attention. "At the very least, you'll be looking over your shoulder the rest of your life. Either way, it probably won't turn out good for you."

"So, I should just forget about it."

"For now, yes. Do you want to throw your life away for that asshole?"

Ty sat in silence for a while. Then, finally, he said, "I guess you're right." He picked up his glass and took a long, hard drink.

I was relieved, but I knew that Ty wouldn't forget what happened that day. It wasn't out of the question that one day he would take his revenge and kill Bruno.

Overall, Ty was someone who I could always count on, especially when it came to committing acts of violence, and we also made some money together.

▼ ▼ ▼

Louie "The Shoe" Santos: The first time I met Louie, I was around twelve years old. He was five years older than me and used to come to my father's store with Bruno, who was mentoring him. Louie is a larger-than-life guy who is half-Italian and half-Dominican. Had he been a full-blooded Italian, he would have gotten his button. Back then, you had to be of pure Italian blood to get straightened out. Today, if your father is Italian and your mother isn't, you can become a Made guy.

Louie was nicknamed "The Shoe" because he was a flashy dresser and always had nice, shiny shoes. More often than not, he kept a gun tucked away in his waistline. Louie wasn't a big guy, but he wasn't afraid to fight with his hands or a weapon if he had to. We would often see Louie in the company of a lady, and he had many kids who claimed his last name. Louie spent a lot of time with bosses like Skyball, Bruno, Baba, and Delevo. The guys at the top liked him, and he would do whatever they asked, even if it meant he had to break someone's legs with a bat.

When Louie wasn't selling pizza at his shop, he moved kilos of coke with me. He was also a key bookmaker for Bruno, and he did some loan-sharking, which he never liked. Nevertheless, we made some real money together over the years and had a lot of fun spending it. Every year, we flew to Vegas for the Super Bowl, blowing hundreds of thousands in a matter of days. To this day, we are still good friends.

▼ ▼ ▼

Ralphie Santaniello: I have known Ralphie since we were around six. We went to grammar school together at Mount Carmel in the South End. But, unlike me, Ralphie grew up in a Mafia family. His father Amedeo was Bruno's closest ally and Ralphie called him Uncle Al.

Throughout the years Ralphie always had the nicest cars. It wasn't unusual to see him driving a Cadillac, Mercedes, or a Corvette. But unfortunately, he also enjoyed partying with the ladies, and his partying would often get out of control. In the end, I had to break off my business relationship with him because he was draining tens of thousands out of our street kitty. His cocaine habit was too costly, and I considered it theft. With every line he snorted, I was losing money, and I didn't appreciate losing money.

At the time, Ralphie, Anthony Scibelli, and I were the coke kings of Springfield. We were moving a couple of keys a week and bringing in a ton of cash. Ralphie was also selling pot with us and doing some loan-sharking and illegal gambling. Later in his criminal career, he was arrested for extortion and would get five years in prison. For a short while, Ralphie worked for Bruno doing some sports gambling and loan-sharking, but after a couple of years Bruno bounced him. Most of us found him to be unreliable, and because of that, I had a couple of run-ins with him. It wasn't that he was a bad guy; he just let his partying get out of control, and in our life, that is detrimental to business success.

In many cases, this behavior can cause people to get sloppy and lose perspective, which can bring on the heat. Ralphie was arrested for racketeering after he was caught on tape talking business. The Organized Crime Task Force had bugged his house and uncovered incriminating evidence, which got him a three-year sentence. When all was said and done, I made a lot of money with Ralphie, but it could have been a lot more.

▼ ▼ ▼

Ryan "Shakes" Fattini: What drew me to Ryan was that he was a quiet guy. He was around five years younger than me and a couple of inches shorter. I first met Ryan while he sat at the bar at Angelina's restaurant that I owned with Frankie Depergola. I took to him straightaway, and after that he was around me quite a bit—I was mentoring him. He was labeled "Shakes" by Freddy because he shook his leg nervously when he was sitting down.

Ryan's father, a bank robber, was shot and killed by the police. His legacy of crime would be passed down to his son. Ryan was from Agawam and worked as a pizza-maker until he began his criminal career when he was around twenty-one years old. It was soon after that when we met at my restaurant. I had him pick up several pounds of weed in New York and Boston and transport it back to Connecticut. We used to store the weed at his mother's and uncle's houses—along with some of our weapons.

What I liked about Ryan was that he was low-key and very reliable. He didn't drink, smoke, or take drugs and knew how to keep his mouth shut. Ryan was a tough kid and wouldn't hesitate to lock horns with anyone. He was small and compact, like a bull, and he often carried a gun—this ended up getting him into trouble. A guy cut him off on the highway, which turned into a road-rage situation. Ryan shot at the guy's car several times, and the guy took down Ryan's plate number and turned him in to the police. He was later convicted and sentenced to two years in prison.

Ryan spent around eight years working with me, and we did quite well together. After I became a Made guy, he moved to Vegas, where he began a short-lived career counting cards at blackjack tables. He was good at it and made a lot of money. Unfortunately, the casinos eventually caught on to his game and had him blackballed. Counting cards isn't a crime, but they will banish a player and spread the word to other casinos when they suspect trickery. Some casinos have been known to treat card-counters a little rough while showing them the door. Eventually, these grifters will run out of black-jack tables to play at.

After a while, I lost touch with Ryan and haven't heard from him since. I hope he is doing well.

CHAPTER 10

Al Bruno was a very manipulative character. He used to keep guys in his crew loyal through promises of straightening them out. These young guys who dreamt of becoming a Made soldier in the Genovese family would do anything Bruno told them to do. The reality is the majority of those promises would go unrealized. Bruno had no intention of conducting a gun-and-knife ceremony with his guys. He knew if he Made a guy, he would lose control over them, and Bruno was a control freak.

I had a love-hate relationship with Bruno. While playing golf with my father, he used to ask, "Why does Bingy always have to go against the grain?" Looking back, I think he liked me because he saw his younger self in me. On the other side of that coin, he saw a kid who was a rebel and hard to control. My father and Bruno spent a lot of time together at the store and on the golf course. Their respect was mutual, even though my father wasn't in the game.

My dad was disappointed when I told him I had received my button. I could hear it in his words and see it in his eyes. Like every son, I wanted my father to be proud of me—I'm not sure he ever was. The day I told him, he looked me in the eye and said, "Why did you do that?" We loved each other dearly, but I often wonder if he would have had a brighter gleam in his eye if I had become a doctor, an accountant, or a successful businessman.

Left to right:
Bruno, Cosimo
Cordi, Louie
Santos, and Victor
Ferrentino

As I stated, I began my business dealings with Bruno running backroom casino gambling, which eventually blossomed into running numbers, sports gambling, loan-sharking, extortion, Vegas gambling junkets, and truck hijacking. Selling coke and pot was something I always did on the side without Bruno's knowledge or approval. I also kept my grifting of drug dealers from him. If he knew I was robbing drug dealers, he would believe that I was in the drug business, which was forbidden.

Bruno was very a greedy guy. He was always looking for ways to beat us out of our cut in the deals we put together. I would do all the work, yet I was expected to fork over 50 percent. And when it came time to split up the cash, he would say, "We need to give a piece to this guy and that guy," or "I need to send something to New York." In the end, I'd be lucky to end up with 30 percent, and Bruno would pocket seventy.

I believe that his greed had a lot to do with his demise. It came to the point where Bruno was shaking down many businesses owned by Italians in the city, and this didn't sit well within the Italian community. We are expected to take care of our own, not bleed them. He was extorting money from the owners of the Mardi Gras strip club, Shabooms dance club, Cocktails bar, Red Rose restaurant, La Fiorentina Pastry Shop, and many more. His biggest shakedowns came from independent bookmakers. In his mind, nobody had a right to take bets in the city without his approval—especially when they weren't giving him a taste.

With all of Bruno's faults, his charisma was the one thing he had going in his favor. He was likable, especially to regular citizens and legitimate businesspeople. He was also friendly with politicians like Mayor Mike Albano, who would often do him favors. In one case, Albano lobbied and won federal grants, which allowed Bruno to renovate his buildings on Worthington Street. He was friendly with State Representative Cheryl Rivera and State Senator Linda Melconian. Bruno would cozy up to judges, federal agents, cops, and lawyers with an agenda that they could be of use to him in the future. Pretty much any relationship Bruno nurtured was because he would get something out of it in the future. He was a master manipulator.

Bruno and I would often take rides to Boston, Providence, New York, New Jersey, and Philadelphia to meet with wiseguys from the Genovese family and other associated families. He was good at building relationships with other criminals. That's something I would learn to excel at as well. We met with Carlo Mastrototaro of Worcester and Luigi Manocchio of Providence. In Boston, we had sit-downs with Patriarca family members Carmen DiNunzio, Peter Limone, and Freddy Simone. At one point, we took a long drive south to meet with guys in the Philadelphia Lucchese family.

Every year during Christmas, we would drive to New York and meet at Il Mulino's restaurant in White Plains. The eatery was owned by the family of Vincent "The Chin" Gigante, who was the boss of our family. Gigante used to evade prosecution by acting like a guy with dementia and mental illness. He would roam the streets in his bathrobe and slippers, mumbling to himself and he had himself hospitalized twenty-five times for schizophrenia. In the end, the former professional boxer was sentenced to twelve years for conspiracy to commit murder and racketeering. Unfortunately, Gigante missed his calling; he should have been in Hollywood and could have won an Academy Award for his acting abilities. Instead, he died in prison at the age of seventy-seven from heart disease.

▼ ▼ ▼

Bruno and I would drive down with a van filled with gifts for Mario Gigante, Pat DeLuca, and other wiseguys in the family. We spent upwards of sixty to seventy thousand on expensive scotch, cognac, wine, Cuban cigars, meat, and cheese. This helped keep Bruno on good terms with the New York goodfellas. Bruno used to say, "A few gifts every year keeps the vultures from asking me for cash payments, and it keeps me in good graces with them." Bruno also gave a lot of gifts to politicians, judges, lawyers, and prominent businesspeople in our area. He was extremely skilled at using a carrot and a stick.

I learned a lot while running with Bruno, and one of the most important lessons I learned is that treachery can get you killed.

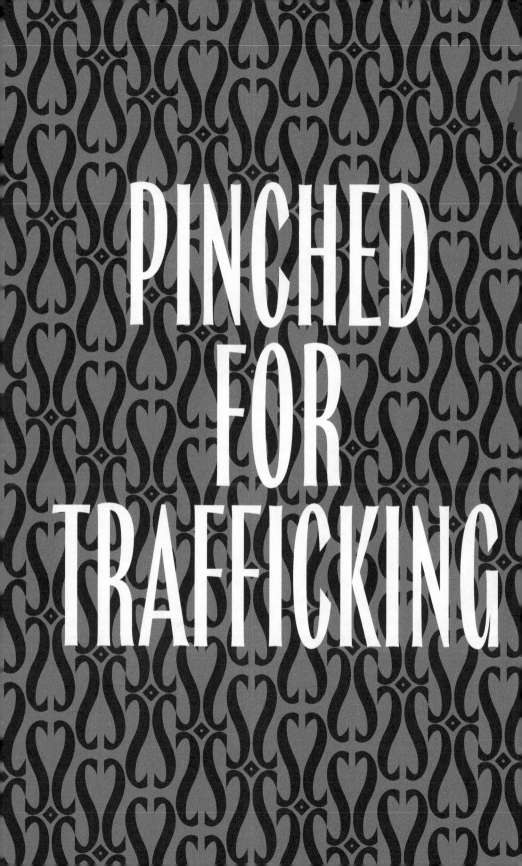

CHAPTER 11

In the mid-1990s, I was selling huge amounts of marijuana, and I was considered one of the biggest traffickers in New England. If you were smoking weed in the Northeast back then, you probably got it through me. I was buying and selling around two hundred pounds a week on average. My sources came from many different circles, including Jamaicans from Hartford, guys from Whitey Bulger's crew in Boston, and mobsters in the Bonanno family out of New York. We would meet at places of business, guys' apartments, and sometimes in remote settings, moving the product between automobiles. After building trust and a working relationship with my suppliers, I would have my shipments fronted and I would pay them later. The quality of the weed didn't matter to me because I had customers on both spectrums—people who wanted high-end weed, and some who wanted ragweed. I would pay around five to six thousand a pound for the quality weed, and for the ragweed the cost was only two to five hundred. On average, I was taking in around sixty thousand a week. The low-end weed was more profitable and put more money in my pocket, but some customers only wanted the high-end product and were willing to pay a premium for the best stuff on the market. Although two-hundred pounds took up a lot of space, it would come in thirty-pound compacted bales wrapped in cellophane and aluminum tape.

Sometimes, the product was vacuum sealed, which would help mask the strong odor. I used to store the product at a couple of my associates' places and occasionally inside freezers at my house. The customers I trusted would come to my house, and I would supply them with anywhere from five to forty pounds. I seldom sold less than that because I had to move large quantities to keep the flow coming in from my suppliers.

One of my customers, Yassir Bakr, was buying and selling weed and moving large quantities of cocaine. He was one of those Middle-Eastern type of guys who you might think would stick a dagger into your spine when you weren't looking. One afternoon, he called me and said that twelve pounds out of the forty I sold him were no good, so I told him to come by the house, and I'd swap them out for different ones. A few hours later he came by, and I gave him twelve new pounds, and he left.

That same night there was a knock at my door, and when I opened it, the police were there asking me if the Jeep Cherokee parked outside was mine. I told them it was, and they said they had information that it was involved in a hit-and-run accident. I responded by stating that wasn't possible because I was the only one driving it and I hadn't been in any accidents. But one of the cops suggested we go and look, so I followed them outside. After walking around the car and seeing no indication of an accident, two plain-clothes cops came out of nowhere with guns drawn and cuffed me. They took me back into the house and sat me down in the living room. At that point, a narcotics officer, Steve Kent, showed me the warrant to search my house. As I read through the warrant, I read that a confidential informant stated he had bought marijuana from me at my house within the past twenty-four hours. I cooperated with them as they ransacked our home; I needed to keep my wife and kids calm. I asked them if we could get them something to drink or if they wanted a snack, but they declined. In the basement, they uncovered forty pounds of weed inside a large box and they found handgun ammunition. I was relieved that they didn't look above the ceiling tiles in the basement, where I had four hundred and fifty thousand in cash. After the search was concluded, I was taken to the Springfield police station and booked.

The judge had set bail at a hundred thousand, and I was released the following day. I thought about the four people who had come by my house in the past twenty-four hours to buy weed. There was Ryan, Rocco, Ilamo, and

In court with my lawyer
Vincent Bongiorni

Yassir. Out of the four guys who came by, the only one I suspected was Yassir. The other three I trusted and knew to be solid guys.

Two days later, Yassir called me and asked for a meeting, so I agreed. At the meeting, he seemed extremely nervous, and when I told him I wasn't ruling him out as the rat, his color changed, and his jittering increased. During our conversation, he indicated he knew about the twenty-four-hour time frame stated in the warrant. He said he had a friend on the police force who was protecting him and giving him information. Yassir also indicated that he might know who set me up, stating the same guy had tried to set him up in the past. At that point, I knew he was a police informant because he would not have known how the warrant read unless he was directly involved in the operation and my arrest. At that very moment, I began plotting how I would kill him, but I had to wait until he paid me the money he owed me. The next day, I met with Yassir again, and he paid me ninety thousand dollars in cash.

A few days passed by and Yassir called and asked me if I was still moving the product or lying low, and I told him I was still open for business. We arranged to make a deal, but I said to him that, under the circumstances, I couldn't front the weed and would need the sixty-thousand up front. He agreed, and I told him to meet me that night at six o'clock at a gas station near Sixteen Acres.

I decided to use my sister's car instead of my Jeep for the exchange, and as I sat waiting, I watched him drive right past me. He must have been looking for my Jeep and didn't notice me in the Nissan. I began waving at him, and he finally spotted me and drove over, and I signaled for him to follow me. As I stopped at a light, I noticed an undercover detective car pull up alongside Yassir, and they had words. The cops didn't catch on to the fact that I was in front of them in a Nissan—they were also expecting a Jeep. The light changed, and I accelerated, and I saw the cops take a left turn—Yassir was still behind me. He followed me to the Red Rose restaurant, and we parked in the back parking lot and he gave me the cash. I told him I had to be careful now and that I would hide the weed at a specific Dairy Mart behind the dumpster.

A half-hour later, I got a call from Yassir saying the package wasn't there, and with a huge smile on my face, I hung up without speaking.

Right after Yassir had given me the money, I drove to a friend's place of business and asked him to hold it for me, and then I went home. A half-hour after I hung up on him, there was a knock at my door, and I answered to find Yassir standing on my front steps.

"Anthony, there was nothing behind the dumpster."

"I don't know what you're talking about," I said, thinking he was probably wearing a wire.

"What do you mean? You were supposed to leave the weed for me."

"I'm sorry, I don't know what you mean. I don't know anything about any weed."

He just stood looking at me with a blank stare. I wanted to put a gun to his head and rip his shirt off to locate a wire.

"Okay, can I get my money back?"

"What money? I don't know what you're talking about. Did you bump your head or something? You're not making any sense."

At that point, he knew it was a lost cause. He gave me a look of disgust, and he walked away. I figured some of the sixty grand may have been police department funds, and if that were the case, they would be super pissed-off. Luckily, I never heard anything more about the money from anyone. I was happy I had gotten some payback on Yassir, but it wasn't enough—he was a rat and needed to die like a rat.

When the case went to court, I was looking at getting sentenced to a couple of years, so I hired Attorney Vinny Bongiorni, who was regarded as the best lawyer in town. Vinny had done his homework and discovered that Yassir was an informant for Officer Steve Kent in the Springfield Police's Narcotics Bureau. He also learned that Yassir's protection from the Springfield Police didn't hold any weight with the Massachusetts State Police. The State Police had recently arrested him for various charges, including trafficking cocaine in a school zone, illegally possessing a firearm and auto-insurance fraud. Vinny informed the judge that he believed Yassir was an informant for the Springfield Police and that the State Police had recently arrested him for trafficking cocaine in a school zone. Vinny also told the judge that the Springfield narcotics officers had been coddling him as their informant with the knowledge that he was committing felonies.

The judge sat silently for a few seconds while staring at the officer.

"Officer Kent, is this true?"

"No," Kent mumbled.

"Was your informant recently arrested by the State Police for selling cocaine?" The judge asked.

Kent hesitated. "Yes."

"You will need to produce the informant," the judge demanded.

"Judge, I can't do that." Kent said in a tone of conviction.

"Why not?"

"Because his identity needs to remain confidential to protect the integrity of ongoing investigations and for his safety as well."

"If you can't produce the informant, I will have to dismiss the case."

"Judge, do what you have to do, but I can't divulge the identity of my informant," Kent said with a hint of contempt.

"Case dismissed."

The sound of the gavel was music to my ears. I knew I had dodged a bullet in court, but I hadn't forgotten about Yassir and his betrayal.

Two days later, I called Yassir and told him that now that the case was over, I could pay him back the sixty grand I owed him, and we could resume business. I asked him to meet me behind the abandoned Friendly's restaurant on Sumner Avenue. It was an excellent place to kill someone with the highway on-ramp just up the street for a quick escape.

Freddy, Louie, Ryan, and I were planning on clipping him around 8 p.m. in the parking lot behind the building. We also learned that Yassir had ratted on Giuseppe "Caga Sotto" Manzi, and he was also supposed to come along to take part in the hit. But Manzi backed out at the last minute. That's how he got the nickname "Caga Sotto," which means "shit your pants." Every time we were going to do any kind of violence, Manzi would run to the bathroom and ultimately chicken out. He was one of those guys who liked to act like a big-shot mobster, but he had no balls.

When I pulled up to the abandoned parking lot, Louie got out of his car and walked over.

"That piece of shit has the State Police here," Louie said, gesturing to an undercover car parked in the far corner of the rear lot.

Freddy and Ryan sat in their car, watching from a distance as Yassir pulled up and parked his car. The plan was that Louie would shoot him in the head, and we would hit the highway and head south to Connecticut to secure an alibi.

As Yassir got out of his car and began walking toward us, another State Police car pulled into the rear lot and parked. There appeared to be at least five cops who just sat watching from a distance. At that point, Freddy and Ryan drove off.

"So, you set me up again?" I said to Yassir, who was now standing outside my car window.

"No, what are you talking about?" He stammered.

"The cops are parked right over there. You brought them here, you fuckin' rat."

"I didn't bring them. I'm not a rat," he said as his face changed to a paler shade.

"You're a scumbag rat," Louie said.

"I'll deal with you later," I said, and we drove away.

We were never able to get Yassir because he was being protected until he was sentenced to a year in prison. He should have been sentenced to at least ten years, but the DA was lenient because he had helped them prosecute many cases as an informant. It reminds me of the Whitey Bulger–John Connolly relationship, where Bulger was free to continue committing murders as long as he was informing for the FBI. Although Bulger was committing murder and Yassir was only trafficking drugs, it was the same concept, unethical and, in some instances, illegal. I figured that in the end it would catch up with Yassir, just like it did with many police informants.

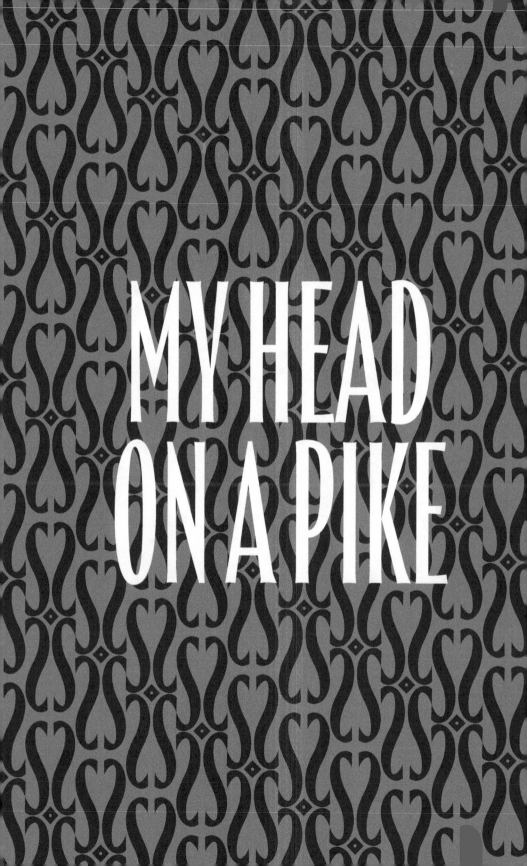

CHAPTER 12

When Bruno discovered I was trafficking large amounts of marijuana, he was furious. I figured it was for two reasons: he wasn't getting a cut of the profits, and he was attempting to maintain the old-school mentality that selling drugs was dangerous for the family. But it really depended on the family. The Bonnanos were not as opposed to drug dealing as the Genoveses were.

Sentences handed down for drug trafficking tended to be very severe—therefore, people were more likely to cooperate, which was extremely risky to the family foundation. Drug dealers could not be trusted to keep their mouths shut when looking at doing hard time.

Skyball Scibelli was the boss of Springfield, and he had made it clear on many occasions that he wouldn't tolerate drug dealers in his organization. He had threatened to kill anyone who broke the rule.

One summer afternoon, Louie Santos and I were driving down the street in the South End in a large van filled with two hundred pounds of weed we had just picked up. Skyball was standing in front of Milano's on Main Street, and he spotted us and waved us over. We reluctantly pulled over, and he told us to give him a ride, and he got in.

The smell was so potent from the bales of weed in the rear that we could smell it in the cab. I was nervous that Skyball would smell it and tell us to

Standing left to right: Jake
Zanoit, Freddy Geas, me,
Jimmy Najoleari

Seated left to right: Victor Bruno,
Louie Santos, and Talal Soffan

open the back of the truck. If that happened, we both figured we were dead men walking. Luckily, he didn't notice because I lit a cigar as he got in the truck. After we dropped him off, I turned to Louie, and we both agreed how fortunate we were that the cigar masked his sense of smell. I was pretty sure Skyball would have set an example out of us. If he didn't kill us, we would have been badly maimed.

Bruno was cursing me up and down regarding my drug-trafficking arrest. He told Louie that he had proposed me to become a Made guy and that Bruno's neck was now in a guillotine for allowing one of his guys to sell drugs. He said if it came down to it, he wouldn't take the fall and he would whack me before Skyball went after him. I knew Bruno was a guy who ran his mouth off to show his power and blow off steam, so I let it roll off my shoulders. When my father pulled me aside and said that Bruno told him he should kill me I realized Bruno was serious. I told my father to tell Bruno to go and fuck himself; if he had something to say to me, he should say it to my face, not through my father. My dad begged me to calm down and be very careful—that I was dealing with dangerous people. I was really upset that Bruno pulled my dad into it. He wasn't involved in the Mafia, and he should have been kept out of it. Bruno was out of line. At that point, I was banished from being around anyone associated with the family.

▼ ▼ ▼

Shortly after Bruno threatened my father with my murder, he entered the store. When he arrived, I was in the back room, and he told my father that I owed him eighty grand. He said he was sent to collect a debt that I owed Baba for sports betting—which was true. I ended up working out my debt with Baba, but I didn't give Bruno a nickel.

The two years I was shelved from working with anyone in the Springfield area ended up being some of the best years of my life. I was making connections all over the Northeast, including Eugene "Rooster" Onofrio of New Haven, and we worked together through his partner, Chicky, in marijuana, cocaine, ecstasy, and sports gambling. I bought pounds of weed through Dave Smith in South Boston. He was affiliated with the Winter Hill Gang, run by Whitey Bulger. In New York, I was doing business with Joe Gallo of the Gambino family and Johnny Spirito of the Bonanno family, selling weed and doing sports gambling. I also cultivated my relationship with the Patriarca family out of Providence and Boston. Even though they were at odds with the Springfield wiseguys, I didn't take sides—I needed as many friends as possible if I was going to make a lot of money.

During this time, I bought into the Club Blu nightclub in Hartford, and I was a 30-percent partner. The dance club was rocking. We were making a ton of money, and I was mingling with the young ladies—banging them two at a time. While this was happening, I took many trips to Vegas, where I went on gambling sprees, blowing hundreds of thousands of dollars, fucking many hot girls, and eating and drinking at the finest restaurants—life was good.

▼ ▼ ▼

After Bruno got out of prison in 1998, he told Louie he wanted to see me. It had been two years since I was out on my own, and I was doing great. I met him at his restaurant Cara Mia, and he brought me to the basement, where he began to tell me how I put him in a bad situation by selling drugs. I responded by denying it, stating they weren't my drugs. Bruno asked me if I wanted to start coming around him again and that he would give me 25 percent of loan-sharking and sports betting. I told him I would return, but I wanted 50 percent—he reluctantly agreed. I knew I was going to do all the work, and 25 percent wasn't going to cut it—and looking back, I was right.

I connected with Donny Pepe and Dave Cecchetelli and I had them conduct sports betting while I continued running my other businesses—I was raking in the cash.

The problem was that I was a degenerate gambler, betting upwards of a half million a week on sports. I had to convince Donny and Dave to go along with my newly devised scheme to cover my ass. I was placing bets with them using fictitious names, and when I went into the hole three hundred thousand, I cooked the books, making it appear that the fake people who were betting were on a winning streak. This is how I got out of paying what I owed. I knew if Bruno ever found out, I was a dead man. In the beginning, my head was on a pike. I was a hero in the end, but things were about to take a menacing turn.

CHAPTER 13

The history of the Manzi family goes back to the old country. Quindici was a small town in southern Italy with fewer than three thousand people. As a young man, Tony Manzi was caught in a Mafia war between the Cava and the Graziano families. He sided against the more powerful Cava family and joined with the Grazianos, where he was a low-level associate. After the Cavas shot up his house, he struck back, shooting at the boss of the Cava family as he rode on a motorcycle with another guy down a country road. The bike flipped over, and Tony walked up and shot one of the two guys point blank, killing him. The other guy ran away into the woods and escaped. At that point, Tony knew he had to get his family out of the country because the guy who got away was the boss of the Cava family, and he would be coming after Tony and his family.

Tony moved his family to America, settling in Springfield. He bought a pizza shop on Main Street, where he continued his criminal activities by selling cocaine with his brother Carmine. In the mid-1980s, Tony and Carmine were arrested for trafficking cocaine and sentenced to prison—Tony received five years and Carmine got three. When Tony got out of prison, he was deported back to Italy. Tony's wife and sister were running the shop while he was away, and they were aware of his drug dealings; and eventually, they became part of it. They continued the drug dealing and the restaurant business was a good cover for their illegal activities.

In 1991, Tony returned to Springfield illegally and he continued working at the pizza shop—picking up where he had left off. His brother Carmine worked at a barber shop on Main Street, and he was shaving and cutting the hair of many local wiseguys.

I met Tony in the early Nineties, and he took a liking to me. Soon after, we began doing business together, and I was selling cocaine along with his son Giuseppe. Tony was a pretty tough guy; he had killed a guy in Italy, and he spent five years in prison. Giuseppe, however, was the opposite of his father. He was soft and had no inclination for violence, and he had never seen the inside of a prison. Ultimately, he earned the nickname "Shit-your-pants Manzi."

As time passed, I began selling marijuana, providing weed for Tony and his family to sell on the street. Tony had given me a handgun as a gift, and he told me I should always carry a gun, just like he did. Most of my dealings were through Giuseppe, and I was fronting him a hundred pounds at a time. I took him under my wing, allowing him to move from a shithole apartment into an upscale place. We made a ton of money together, selling hundreds of pounds a month, and our friendship grew. As my wedding day approached, I asked him to be an usher at my wedding party, and he accepted.

Bruno never liked Tony. He didn't like the Manzis at all. Bruno was a guy who never took well to outsiders who didn't pay tribute to him. The Manzis weren't connected to any families in America. They were Italian, and they were making money illegally, and Bruno was pissed that he wasn't getting a cut of the profits. He didn't like how they paraded around like they were big-time Springfield mobsters, yet they didn't have to cut their teeth as he had. The Manzis had never earned their bones, and the word on the street was that Bruno dropped a dime on Tony, and soon after, he was deported back to Italy again.

After many months of Giuseppe and I conducting a successful drug operation together, Giuseppe became greedy and started getting some of his weed from other sources. He was buying it at a lower price, which forced me to drop my prices even lower to remain competitive. Then he started approaching my customers and selling them weed that he was getting from other suppliers. When I approached him about his betrayal, he denied it. My threats of hurting him fell on deaf ears. I didn't act on them because I was still selling him several pounds a week and was still making good money. After a while, I began playing his game, and I was stealing his customers behind his back. That's when things started to turn south for us. He had a very short memory and forgot that I got him started and pulled him out of near poverty. His treachery pissed me off considering all I'd done for him.

In the meantime, Skyball had become friendly with Giuseppe's Uncle Carmine. He used to get his haircut at his shop, and eventually, Carmine began working for Skyball doing sports betting and loan-sharking. The Manzis had finally found a connection with a local Made guy, which went right to Carmine's head. Now, he was talking shit on the streets, bragging that he was tight with Skyball and shouldn't be messed with. He was constantly throwing Skyball's name around and it began to metastasize to the rest of the Manzi family like a malignant cancer.

The bad blood between Giuseppe and me was not an exclusive issue. Freddy and Ty's uncle, who owned a jewelry store, had borrowed thirty grand from Giuseppe's Uncle Carmine, and he was charging him 5 percent interest a week. It really bothered Ty that a Manzi was beating his uncle out of six thousand a month in interest alone. To make things worse, Carmine's son Joe was married to Ty and Freddy's cousin, so they were related to the Manzis through marriage. Another thing that bothered Ty and Freddy was that Giuseppe used to walk around like a big shot telling people, "Do you know who my father is?" The Geas brothers had earned their bones on the street and in prison, and they felt Giuseppe hadn't. That, combined with his cocky attitude, rubbed them the wrong way.

In 2001, Freddy and Ty had ten pounds of weed fronted to them by Giuseppe, and they never paid him back. Ty believed that Giuseppe had ratted him out a few years earlier when Ty got arrested for selling weed. There was no proof, but he strongly felt that Giuseppe had dropped a dime on him. Ty had it out for Giuseppe, and he was prodding him at every opportunity. Ty smashed in the windows at his restaurant, and he used to go to his house and try to get Giuseppe to come out—but he wouldn't. Ty continued his reign of terror by bad-mouthing Giuseppe on the streets and ranting that he was going to kill him. Ty had a street reputation as a crazy, tough guy who wouldn't hesitate to take anyone out. Giuseppe was scared to death of him. He knew Ty was gunning for him, and he wasn't sleeping well.

Tony Capua, Giuseppe's first cousin, was also in the drug-dealing business and was stupid enough to front the Geas brothers fifty pounds of quality weed. When it came time for Capua to collect the hundred-and-fifty thousand, the Geas brothers weren't responding. Finally, after several weeks, Freddy told Capua they had his money and agreed to go to his house and pay him. Once inside the house, Ty picked up Capua and body-slammed him on the floor, knocking the wind out of him. Freddy walked over, chambered a round in his semi-automatic handgun, and placed the barrel of the gun against Capua's head. A puddle formed on the floor as Capua begged for his life. Freddy told him they weren't going to pay him the money. But if Capua set them up for a buy with his supplier, they would pay him his money after they robbed the guy. In a state of panic, Capua agreed, and Ty told him if he said anything to his mother or anyone else, they would kill him and his mother.

Capua's mother was also in the marijuana business. The meeting ended with Freddy pistol-whipping Capua over the head.

▾ ▾ ▾

A few days later, the Manzis had a birthday party, and Freddy and Ty were invited because it was their cousin's kid. Capua's mother was also there, giving the Geas brothers dirty looks. At that point, they were pretty confident that her son had told her about what had happened the day Freddy put a gun to his head. This didn't sit well with Freddy and Ty because they had clearly warned Capua not to tell anyone what they did, including his mother.

It turned out that Capua was working for Emilio Fusco, a Made guy under Baba Scibelli. Fusco went to see Freddy and told him that it was his weed that they had stolen and that he and Ty owed him a hundred-and-fifty grand. Freddy responded by telling Fusco he didn't get any weed from Capua, that he knew it was against the rules to be involved in drugs, and that a guy could get whacked for violating it.

Giuseppe Manzi and my sister Angela at my wedding

Bruno hated Fusco and was pissed off that Baba made him a member of their elite society. He wanted to get permission to clip Fusco, and when he heard that Freddy robbed Fusco of his pot, this was an excellent opportunity for him. Bruno went to Freddy, asking him if he bought weed from Fusco, and Freddy told him he had gotten it from Capua, not Fusco. Freddy didn't want to get into a feud between two Made guys. He knew it wouldn't be good for his long-term health. In order to make Bruno happy, Freddy and Ty gave Bruno five thousand out of the money they made from Capua's fifty pounds, and he was good with that. As far as Bruno was concerned the situation was closed.

The common denominator in the dissension with all the players involved was Giuseppe Manzi—he was toxic. At least that's how Freddy and Ty saw it. I stayed clear of all the bullshit between the Manzis, the Capuas, and the Geas brothers. I was not inclined to get in the middle of all that drama.

I received a call from Giuseppe asking me to meet him at his restaurant, and I reluctantly agreed. When I got there, he began pleading with me to help him because Ty was harassing him to no end. I told him Ty was my friend, and I didn't want to get involved, so he called Italy and got his father on the phone. He knew I liked and respected his dad, and he thought the call might help change my mind. I got on the phone with Tony, and he began begging me to help his family by asking Ty to back off, and I responded by telling him I wouldn't do it. I also understood how close Giuseppe was to his cousin, Tony Capua, and now they had a common enemy—the Geas brothers. I didn't like or trust Giuseppe or his cousin and I was close with the Geas brothers, so this was an easy call for me to make.

It was about a week later that I received a call from a friend of mine, Dave Cecchetelli. He went on to tell me that his nephew Mike, the leader of the Springfield chapter of the Latin Kings gang, told him Capua approached two of his gang members asking them to do a hit for money. He said Capua wanted to hire them to kill Freddy and Ty Geas. I asked Dave to set up a meeting with Mike, and the next day, I was at his house with Freddy and Ty. Mike went on to tell us exactly what happened with the proposed targets, with Freddy and Ty keenly listening. He assured us his guys would not take the contract against the Geas brothers, and it was obvious that Ty had a look in his eye that told a story of pure hatred and revenge. Freddy was a bit more reserved and suggested that Mike's guys kill Capua instead for the same amount of money. Mike agreed, and the next day Freddy, Ty, and I met with Mike and gave him a gun to do the job—stating we would pay the hitters once the job was done.

As time passed by, Mike continued making excuses on why his Latin Kings crew didn't commit the murder—the hit on Capua never materialized.

▼ ▼ ▼

Tensions were running high between the Geas brothers and the Manzi and Capua families. It was early September of 2003 when Ty got a call from his close friend Brandon Croteau, who later would be the getaway driver for Frankie Roche on the night he shot Al Bruno. Brandon was bartending at Tilly's Pub when Giuseppe walked in with ten of his friends and started abusing him. One guy threw a beer bottle at him, missing his head by inches.

Ty told me what happened at the bar and within minutes we had fifteen guys armed to the teeth and ready to roll. We loaded up three cars and headed down to Tilly's. By the time we arrived, they had left; but soon after, we found out they all went to Giuseppe's family bar, the Civic Pub. We had a couple drinks in us when we loaded back up and drove to the pub. I had a five-iron, Ty had an icepick, and Freddy had a .22 caliber pistol. As we pulled up, we noticed they were all standing outside the entrance to the pub. I figured someone must have tipped them off that we were coming.

We got out of our vehicles and went after them like the Roman army attacking the Barbarians. Except for a couple of our guys, everyone was wielding a weapon. I started swinging my golf club like a maniac, and I looked over and saw Ty stabbing a guy with his icepick. Our guys were hitting people with baseball bats and steel pipes, and then Freddy began firing at them with his handgun. This was when everyone began fleeing like cockroaches. A few of Manzis friends had attempted to fight back but soon realized defeat was inevitable. People ran from the scene in a panic, and I heard someone yell that the cops were on their way. One of Manzi's guys was kicking the shit out of Ty and Freddy's brother Billy Geas, so I swung my five-iron as hard as possible, catching him in the base of the skull. He dropped immediately, and I thought I might have killed him. I helped Billy up and looked around, noticing that Manzi's crew had either fled or were bleeding on the ground. I also noticed that Giuseppe wasn't there; he had disappeared and was probably shitting his pants behind the building.

I told my guys that we had to get out of there fast. As we ran back toward our cars, we could hear the police sirens infiltrating the night air. Freddy disappeared on foot with the gun, and the rest of us piled into our cars and raced off into the night.

A block away, blue lights illuminated the inside of our car, and a siren rang out, so we pulled over. A patrol car stopped us, and the uniformed officers approached with guns drawn. A minute later, another cruiser arrived on the scene, and then several more. The cops had the five of us exit the car and lie on the ground on our stomachs. One of the cops was Vinny Santaniello, the cousin of Jimmy Santaniello, who was connected to the Mob and an owner of the Mardi Gras strip club. Vinny and I went way back, and when he saw me, he came walking over.

"Bingy, what the fuck are you up to?" he asked.

"Nothing," I lied.

"Nothing, really?" he said shaking his head.

"Just out with my friends." If he had looked in the trunk, he would have learned differently. It was packed with clubs, knives, and pipes. We would have been placed in cuffs and hauled off in a New York minute.

"Were you guys just at the Civic Pub? He was pacing in front of the five of us as we lay with heads facing the dirt.

"No." At that point I had resigned myself to the fact that we were going to be arrested, or at least taken back to the scene to be identified and then arrested.

At that moment, a guy came limping over with another cop. I figured the cop must have brought him there from the scene of the mayhem. The guy had been shot in the leg and was bleeding.

"Are these the guys? Were they at the Civic Pub?" The cop asked him.

The guy looked at me and scanned our guys sprawled out on the pavement. He hesitated, and I thought that we were fucked.

"No, these aren't the guys," he said while looking me in the eye.

"Are you sure?" The cop asked. "Take a closer look."

"I'm sure. These guys weren't there."

At that point, they cut us loose, and we drove off as free men. In the end, Freddy put bullets in three guys, and one of them was ours. He accidentally shot one of my crew during the melee. Ty stabbed three guys, including one in the chest who was in critical condition. Several others were beaten badly and taken to the hospital for concussions and lacerations requiring stitches. A couple of our guys had to go for treatment, including our guy who Freddy shot in the head. Luckily, he was just grazed, and it didn't cause any lasting damage.

It was a wild and exhilarating night that I'll never forget. But it wasn't over—the Manzis would begin plotting their revenge.

CHAPTER 14

A couple of days after the fight outside the Civic Pub, I was at my club in Hartford when I got a 911 signal on my beeper. This was a signal I used when someone I was close with had an emergency. It was around midnight when I dialed the number on my beeper that I didn't recognize. My wife Irene picked up the line and she was hysterical. She was using a phone at my neighbor's after fleeing our house with the kids because it wasn't safe. After calming her down, she told me someone shot up our house while she and the kids were sleeping. Irene was with my nine-year-old son and my baby daughter of two months when the shots rang out—luckily, no one was hurt.

After attempting to calm her down, I reassured her I was on my way home and would be there as quickly as possible. Freddy was with me that night, and we sprang to action, along with ten other guys. We raced back to Springfield, driving over a hundred miles an hour. It would normally be a thirty-five-minute drive, we did it in twenty-five. When we arrived at my house, there were cop cars everywhere. The detectives immediately came over and told me my house was hit around twenty-five times, and my front-door glass was shot out. Most of the bullets had struck the lower part of my house, which was made of brick, and this made me believe that the maggots responsible were trying to send a message, not trying to kill anyone. My wife's car also had bullet holes in it as it sat parked in the driveway. The detectives pulled me aside and began questioning me.

"Anthony, do you know who did this?" The tall detective asked with a pen and pad in hand.

"No." I was confident that the Manzis were behind the attack. It was against Mob rules to go after family members or the residence they stayed at. Wives and kids were off-limits, and I figured whoever was responsible wasn't directly connected with a Mob crew. The Manzis weren't part of a local Mafia family—they were renegades.

"Do you have any enemies that you think may have done this?" he asked.

"No." I knew it had to be them. Two days earlier, we shot, stabbed, and beat the shit out of their guys. Who else could it be so soon after the mayhem took place?

"So, you have no idea who may have done this?"

"No, no idea."

"Anthony, this is a nice neighborhood. I live just down the road, and we don't need this kind of shit happening in our neighborhood. A lot of people will be watching this closely, and many of them will be pissed off."

"Yeah, and I'm one of them," I said and walked away.

After calming Irene down, her family and my mother went inside with her and the kids. I walked over to where Freddy and my friends were waiting.

"I need you guys to see if you can find any of the Manzis or their people. Try their restaurant, their houses, or any place they might have gone after shooting up my house."

"What are you going to do?" One of the guys asked.

"What am I going to do?" I stepped in closer to him. "I'm going to kill them all."

While my guys cruised the streets looking for the Manzis, I drove out to meet Dicky Jovilet at his condo in Agawam. Dicky was a good friend and kept a stash of my weapons at his place for occasions like this.

"Are you sure you want to do this?" he asked, and his words hung in the air for a minute. I could see the concerned look in his eyes.

"Dicky, they shot up my house. My wife and kids were in bed sleeping and woke up to bullets shattering the windows," I said through clenched teeth. "Yes, I'm sure."

"Alright. You should just be sure it was them before you start shooting—just saying."

"Who else could it be?" I asked as I took a couple boxes of ammo out of the closet.

"I'm sure Manzi isn't the only enemy you have."

"I suppose not. I hear what you're saying."

I retrieved two AK-47s and two handguns from his place and began plotting my next move.

It was late by the time we began our search for the Manzis, and nobody was to be found at 3 a.m. It was going to have to wait until the next day. It was probably a good thing because I was livid and not thinking too clearly. I was like a mad dog that night, and I would have started shooting if I had spotted one of them. I wasn't sure who the actual shooters were, but I was pretty sure the Manzis were behind it.

The following day, we packed up the family, and I drove them to the Connecticut shore, where I rented a house in Old Saybrook. After settling them in, I returned to Springfield, and Artie Nigro reached out to me. I told him what had happened, and I said I was probably going to kill some people. He told me to wait. He said it was too hot right now and that would bring serious heat down on all of us. Artie promised me if I waited six months, he

Left to right: With
"Little Joe" Manzi,
"Little Johnny," and
Anthony Grasso

would send a hit squad up to clip the guys responsible, and I responded by saying I would think about it. I had no intention of doing that—I wanted revenge *now*.

I spent that entire day looking for Giuseppe but couldn't find him.. I was told he had left the state, which raised a red flag. If he truly was innocent of the shooting, why would he flee the state instead of reaching out for a sit-down to proclaim his innocence. That's what I would do if I were in his situation and wasn't involved in the shooting. I was also looking for some of his closest friends and family members, but nobody was around. Everyone had disappeared.

Several days later, I got a call from Emilio Fusco asking for a meeting, so I agreed. At the meeting, he told me he spoke with Giuseppe, and he told Fusco he had nothing to do with the shooting and wanted to sit down. He asked that I meet with him at his restaurant, and I agreed. I was suspicious about why he waited so long to ask for a meeting after he had fled Massachusetts. I was thinking that he needed time to conjure up a story and wanted to run it by some of his friends.

When we arrived at the restaurant, Freddy and I were carrying the two handguns I had gotten from Dicky's place. Fusco and Felix also came along, and they were probably carrying guns—I wasn't sure. Freddy and I agreed that if there weren't many customers at his place, we would kill Giuseppe on the spot unless he gave us the shooters' names. Unfortunately, several people were eating and ordering lunch, so it wasn't the best situation for a hit.

In the kitchen, I confronted Giuseppe, who denied knowing anything about the shooting. Carmine was also there, denying any knowledge of the attack. Tightly gripping the pistol in my jacket pocket, I told Giuseppe that if he gave me the shooters' names, I wouldn't kill him. I think I smelled shit, and that's when he raced off to the men's room.

As I waited for him, I thought about the scene from *The Godfather* when Michael Corleone came out of the toilet with a gun and began killing people. I soon snapped out of it knowing Guiseppe didn't have the balls to pull a trigger.

When he returned, my finger was on the trigger, and I was ready just in case. Carmine handed me a phone. It was Tony calling from Italy.

"Bingy, Giuseppe didn't have anything to do with the shooting. Nobody from our side did."

"Tony, with all due respect, you can't say that. You're over there, not here. Isn't it ironic that a few days after we had a beef at the pub, and beat the hell out of Giuseppe and his friends, that my house if shot up?"

"It had to be somebody else that has a problem with you; it wasn't us."

"You know the rules. Family is off-limits no matter what."

"Bingy, I treated you like my own son. Our family loves you and wouldn't do anything like this," he said in a whiny tone. "Please don't go after my family."

"Tony, this isn't about you; it's about your kid. You should have had better control over him."

"It wasn't him; you must believe me. He would never do this to you and your family. We will help you find out who did this and we will kill them."

"Don't worry about it. I'll find out on my own."

I hung up, knowing it was bullshit just like when O. J. Simpson said he was going to hire a private investigator to find the killer of his wife and Ron Goldman after being acquitted for stabbing them to death. The whole time he knew he was the guilty one.

The restaurant was beginning to empty, and I whispered to Freddy, "It's clearing out; let's whack them both and get out of here."

We had a couple of guys outside watching the restaurant in case the Manzis tried to ambush us. There was also the possibility that the cops were doing surveillance and waiting to move in for an arrest. Giuseppe was a snake, and it was a real possibility that he was an informant.

Just when we thought it was time to put a couple of bullets in Giuseppe and Carmine's heads, Freddy got a beep from the guys outside. He called them back from the restaurant, and they told him they spotted a couple of undercover cops outside watching the restaurant—so we left.

Four days passed and I was getting impatient. I desperately wanted to find out who shot up my house while my little kids slept in their beds. This was a code that was honored and enforced in the Mafia. We could never go after family—especially kids. What if one of those bullets hit one of my kids in the head? This couldn't go unpunished.

I went to Carmine's barbershop and took him down to the basement. I pulled out my gun and placed it against his temple—he turned white as a ghost.

"Who shot at my house? I know you know who did it!"

"Please, Anthony. I don't know anything about it."

"You're a fucking liar. My house was shot up a couple of days after we beat down your guys at the Civic Pub—so it had to be you. Who else could it be?"

"I don't know, Anthony, but I'll help you find out, and we will get even with them."

"You're a lying piece of shit. My wife and kids were in the house and could have been killed."

"We didn't do it! Why would we shoot at your house? That's not the kind of people we are. We have nothing but respect for you, Anthony."

"I don't believe you. You Manzis are scumbags, and you would make a chickenshit move like this. I should blow your brains out right here."

"Please, Anthony, don't," he cried.

I cocked the hammer back until it clicked, pushing the gun harder against his head, and he closed his eyes. A few seconds later, I slowly released the hammer and stepped back.

"If I find out you had anything to do with this, I'm coming back. Next time, I will pull the trigger."

I left him sitting on the floor in a puddle of his own piss, and I walked out.

▼ ▼ ▼

Ty had been in prison with a guy from Boston who was seriously deranged. He had killed a few people but was never linked to the murders. I sat with him and another guy at a restaurant in Worcester. I produced a photo of Giuseppe and handed it to Ty's friend, who sat across the table along with another crazy-looking guy. They said they wanted twenty thousand to kill Giuseppe, and I agreed to pay them once the hit was done. In the next couple of weeks, they went looking for Giuseppe, armed and ready to take him out. They ate at his restaurant several times, but he was nowhere to be found. To this day, I think I had a mole in my crew because Giuseppe must have been alerted that I put a contract on him—he disappeared. The hitters never got the opportunity to clip him.

At this point, it was open season on Giuseppe. I put the word out that if anyone saw him they were to kill him on sight. He was on the run but had to surface eventually. I would make whoever killed him whole once the deed was finished.

▼ ▼ ▼

Frankie Roche was a complete nutcase. He would ultimately be the guy who shot and killed Al Bruno in Springfield. Freddy had given Roche an AK-47, and he was on the hunt for Giuseppe. He waited outside Giuseppe's restaurant several times, but he never showed up. Word on the street was that Giuseppe was totally stressed out and had dropped a ton of weight. That didn't surprise me because he was always shitting when he was scared—the defecation diet. Ty hated Giuseppe and pressured Roche to find him. He wanted Giuseppe dead so badly he could taste it.

One afternoon Roche was cruising down Main Street and spotted Giuseppe out of the corner of his eye. He was sitting in a car across the street. Roche immediately grabbed his AK-47 and began following him. Once Giuseppe's car stopped, Roche opened fire with his assault rifle, ripping holes into his car. Luckily for Giuseppe, he ducked down onto the floor and wasn't hit. Roche sped off and was never caught.

After the attempted hit on Main Street, Giuseppe crawled into the cracks and didn't come out. I wasn't going to give up on getting him, but another matter suddenly came up: Gary Westerman.

CHAPTER 15

Al Bruno became the boss in 2001, and as time went by, he became more and more greedy. The guys in his crew who were doing all the work were paying Bruno 50 percent or more of the take. He was also pitting one guy against another by spreading rumors, like this guy might be stealing from us, or that guy may be a rat. Bruno was causing a lot of dissension among the ranks, and now that he was the boss of our area, the power went right to his head, and he felt invincible. If Bruno made a buck, he spent a buck. He was a guy who liked to show off that he had a lot of money, and he would eat at the finest restaurants and drink high-end liquor.

Bruno started shaking down many local bars and restaurants to get a cut of their weekly receivables, and this was bringing some heat down on him from law enforcement. He was also moving on to other legitimate businesses, such as CJ's Towing. He had approached the owner of CJ's, Craig Morel, and promised him a city contract for a piece of the business.

▼ ▼ ▼

When 2003 rolled around, the Genovese bosses in New York heard that Bruno was making boatloads of money. The problem was that he wasn't sending anything down to New York. John Bologna was the buffer between the Springfield Crew and the New York guys, and he was bad-mouthing Bruno to the bosses in New York.

At that time, Bruno had a deal in the works to buy shipping containers full of Marlboro cigarettes from China at a reduced rate, and he was going to make millions on this partnership. They needed a port of entry in the United States to make this happen. Ray Ruggiero was a captain in the Genovese family out of Florida. He had secured a deal with the Governor of Maryland by paying him two-hundred-and-fifty-thousand dollars in cash to allow the containers to be shipped through a port in his state. Bruno had told Artie Nigro about the cigarette deal, and Artie then connected Bruno to Ruggiero, who was friendly with the Governor. Bruno paid Ruggiero a quarter of a million dollars for the connection with the governor. They never paid the Governor a dime, and to this day, nobody knows if there ever was a connection between Ruggiero and the Governor in the first place. Ruggiero split the money Bruno gave him with Nigro. The whole deal may have been a scam by Ruggiero and Nigro to get the bribery cash from Bruno to line their own pockets.

After giving the money to Ruggiero, Bruno could never get ahold of him, so he complained to Artie, not knowing that Artie was in on the scheme. Artie kept telling Bruno to work it out with Ruggiero, and Bruno wasn't getting anywhere with him. Finally, Ruggiero told Bruno the money was gone—that he gave it to a Maryland guy who was supposedly connected to the Governor, and he had stolen it. Bruno couldn't get Ruggiero to disclose the guy's name, and Bruno was mad as hell, and he wasn't going to let it die.

At that time, three bosses were running the Genovese family as a panel: Artie Nigro, Larry Dentico, and Mario Gigante—brother of Vincent "The Chin." Bruno was badgering Gigante about being beaten out of the money, and the bosses realized that Bruno had to be dealt with.

Amedeo Santaniello had been friends with Bruno for years, but they had fallen out after Bruno had bounced Amedeo's son Ralphie out of his crew. The former friends had joint ownership in several bars and restaurants, and Amedeo appealed to Mario Gigante for help. He and Gigante had a friendship that went back many years, so Gigante told Bruno he had to pay Amedeo a hundred-and-fifty thousand for his piece of the business, and then Amedeo would walk away. Bruno reluctantly agreed, feeling that he was being fucked over by Amedeo and the bosses from New York—he

Bruno and my mother
Loretta at my son's
Christening

thought he should have paid much less. Bruno was also jealous of Amedeo's relationship with Gigante, and the fact that Amedeo wasn't a Made guy added to his discontent.

Louie Santos was a protégé of Bruno, and he was around Bruno most of the time. Baba Scibelli's two sons-in-law, Michael Cimmino and Johnny Basile, sent word to me and some of our guys that Louie was an informant. I didn't believe them, but word reached New York, and they decided to have Louie whacked. They also thought that Bruno couldn't be trusted if he allowed his guy Santos to pull the wool over his eyes while ratting with the Feds. The New York guys were worried that Santos would tell the FBI and the State Police about the various aspects of illegal activity being conducted in the Greater Springfield area. This would cause major problems and could possibly shut them down. The decision was made to send a message to Bruno by having Santos killed.

I got a call from Emilio Fusco asking for a meeting, and I went to meet with him. He told me that Bruno screwed him, because he was supposed to get a two-year sentence, and when he went to his hearing, they increased it to three years. He said during discovery it was revealed that Bruno had told the FBI that Fusco was a Made guy, and they increased his sentence by another year. He showed me a 302 form that the FBI uses to summarize a statement given to them by an informant. The name on the document was "CI, Adolfo Bruno." The statement read that Bruno gave them the names of all the Made guys in the Greater Springfield area, including Fusco. This was a huge violation of family rules.

I had heard that Bruno and Fusco had a beef earlier that day at La Fiorentina Pastry Shop. It turns out that Fusco confronted Bruno about the 302 form and they had an argument. Those two guys always hated each other for years, and Bruno was pissed off that Baba made Fusco a family member while he was away in prison. Since Bruno didn't know about the ceremony, he couldn't contest it. Bruno was also jealous of the relationship Fusco had with Baba and was generally an insecure person.

Fusco and I reached out to Felix, arranged a meeting, and showed him the form. Felix called John Bologna in New York and revealed to him that Bruno was a rat. Bologna told Felix to immediately drive to New York and bring the form along with him.

After arriving in New York, Felix met with the three bosses of the family, and after seeing the 302 form, they huddled together for a quick chat. A couple of minutes later, Artie walked up to Felix and told him to kill Bruno. At that point, they shelved the killing of Santos. Bruno was a proven rat, and he had to go *now*.

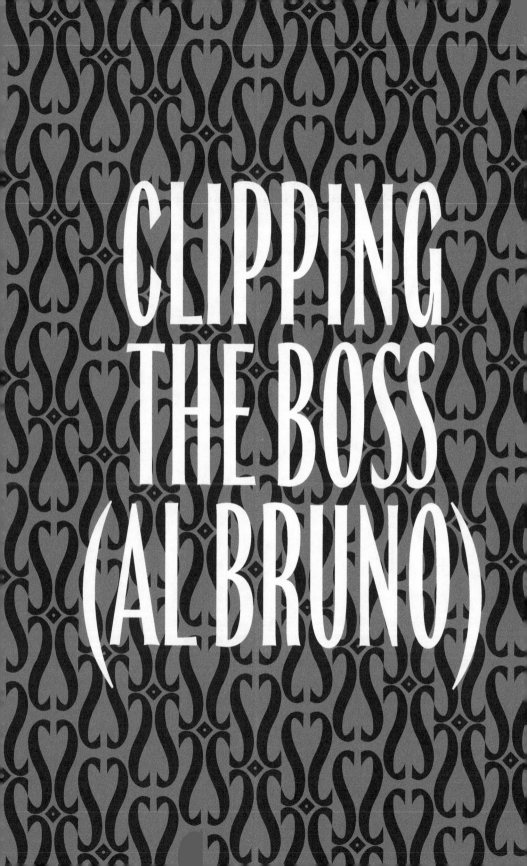

CLIPPING THE BOSS (AL BRUNO)

CHAPTER 16

elix Tranghese was supposed to be the guy leading the effort to make a move on Bruno; however, weeks passed by, and nothing happened. Felix didn't have a crew that was willing and capable of committing a clean murder. Other than perpetrating assault and battery, none of his guys were skilled in serious, violent acts, and none had committed murder.

After thinking it through, the bosses in New York figured asking Felix to do the hit was probably a mistake and would backfire against the organization. They knew I had a crew who had pulled a trigger on at least two people. We shot Dadabo nine times, and we shot some of Manzi's guys and there were whispers that my crew was responsible for Gary Westerman's disappearance. None of us admitted to killing Westerman, but many in the underworld had us pegged as the culprits.

Artie called me for a meeting, and I met him in the Bronx, where we discussed taking Bruno out. He told me he didn't want me to pull the trigger but that I should orchestrate the hit and pull a Houdini afterward. Artie made it clear that he didn't want Bruno's body to ever be found—he was to disappear.

I arranged a meeting with Freddy, Ty, Fusco, and Felix to discuss how and where we would take Bruno out. I wasn't thrilled about killing Bruno because I didn't hate the guy, and I didn't think he deserved to die. But the order came down from the bosses in New York, and if I didn't obey the order to take him out, they would kill me. That's just the way it is in our life.

We had a few ideas on how to make Bruno vanish. The first was to take him to Connecticut for a night of drinking and fine dining—get him drunk and relaxed. Fusco knew a guy in Connecticut who owned a junkyard with a car crusher. We would shoot Bruno in the head in the car and take him to the junkyard and crush the car with him in it. We ultimately decided against that because I couldn't trust that the junkyard guy wouldn't eventually open his mouth. We'd have to kill him as well and that would make it riskier. The second idea was to bring Bruno to my stash house in Agawam for dinner, shoot him at the house, and drop him in a hole we had dug in the backyard. That hole was ultimately occupied by Westerman a few weeks later.

The problem with these methods of execution was that Bruno always had an older guy tagging along with him. Fitzy was Bruno's good friend, who was usually with him until around eight or nine at night. We would have to kill Fitzy too, and we didn't want to do that—he was a good guy and had nothing to do with Bruno's treachery.

We decided we would just have to shoot him when we could and leave his body at the scene. We considered taking him to Max's Tavern on East Columbus Ave. near the Basketball Hall of Fame, When we came out after dinner, he would collect his bullets in the parking lot. I ended up ruling that out because it was a very busy area and there would be a high probability of witnesses.

Freddy Geas came up with the idea to shoot him when he walked out of the Our Lady of Mount Carmel Club at night after drinking and playing cards. He said he knew a guy he thought would take the job.

Frankie Roche was doing time at MCI-Shirley for serious assault convictions, and that's where Freddy first met him, and they became friends. After they were released, they did some jobs together, and Freddy said he thought Roche was crazy enough to commit murder. He suggested we use Roche to do the hit.

Freddy told me about a job that Roche recently did for the owner of Carmelina's restaurant in Hadley. The guy was divorcing his wife and he asked Freddy to tune-up his wife's lawyer who was making his life miserable and was trying to take all his money. Freddy offered the job to Roche for a thousand bucks, and he accepted without hesitation.

Roche knocked on the guy's front door, and when he answered, he beat him senseless with a baseball bat. The attorney spent several days recovering in the hospital with a concussion and broken bones.

Freddy also reminded us that Roche had attempted to kill Giuseppe when he was shooting at him with an AK-47 in broad daylight in downtown Springfield. That took some balls. Freddy was able to convince us that Roche might be the right man for the job.

When Freddy confronted Roche about taking the job, he assured him that once Bruno was out of the picture, they would assume all his business operations and they would give Roche a very nice slice of the pie. A ton of money would be made, and Roche would be a part of any new ventures as well. This was a life-changing situation for Roche, and he couldn't turn it down. It was all bullshit, however, because we had no intention of inviting him to the party.

Roche spent some time watching the Italian club and he said he couldn't get to Bruno. He told Freddy that Bruno always had too many people with him when he came out or Bruno didn't come out of the club as expected. Finally, Freddy told him he had to do it the next day, or else he would just do it himself and Roche would be dead to him. He questioned Roche's commitment and told Roche that he was jeopardizing Freddy's credibility on the street.

The next day, Fusco planted a .45 caliber automatic handgun behind the dumpster at Family Pizzeria for Roche to use for the hit. He figured a gun this powerful should do the job. Bruno had to be killed, and we made it clear that Roche was told to make sure he finished him off—he could not survive the attack.

Frankie Roche

Brandon Croteau drove Roche to the club, and he was told to park across the street while Roche waited for Fusco to beep him when Bruno was about to head outside. Croteau didn't know anything about the murder that was about to unfold.

After he got the beep, Roche waited outside with the gun as Bruno walked out with Frankie Depergola. Bruno was walking to his car when Roche approached him and said, "Hey, Al. I heard you're looking for me?" He raised his gun and shot Bruno five times, and the boss fell to his death with a lit cigar smoldering next to his lifeless body. Roche ran back to the getaway car, and they drove away around 9:15 p.m.

▼ ▼ ▼

The reality is that Bruno was looking for Roche, and he knew it. Roche had picked up the gun a few weeks earlier and he was toting it around with him and terrorizing Michael DeCaro by threatening him at gunpoint.

DeCaro was the son of murdered mobster Victor DeCaro whose body was found in the Connecticut River shot to death in 1972. Victor had been having an affair with Big Nose Sam's wife before disappearing.

It all started at Emo's bar on Locus Street when Roche beat a guy up over a pool table dispute. After being thrown out, Roche and DeCaro returned an hour later and trashed the bar with a baseball bat. About an hour later the pair were drinking at State Street Tavern when Bruno and Fusco came in. Bruno pulled DeCaro outside and told him he needed to convince Roche to make restitution for the damage at Emo's bar because he had an interest in the business.

Roche was against paying Bruno any money for the damage and didn't like that DeCaro was pressuring him, and he beat DeCaro down.

As the days passed and Bruno didn't get any restitution, word on the street was that he was going to go after Roche for the money. The pressure was on DeCaro to convince Roche to pay up and the day before Bruno was killed, Roche pulled the .45 on DeCaro and threatened him. Roche was also upset because DeCaro told Freddy that Roche had punched him out, and Freddy confronted Roche about the beatdown.

Initially, investigators thought the Bruno murder was connected to the Emo's incident and Roche's unwillingness to pay for damages, and that Roche thought Bruno was gunning for him. It wasn't until much later that they uncovered the truth as to why Bruno was killed.

▼ ▼ ▼

The day after Bruno was murdered, Freddy met with Roche at Forest Park and paid him ten thousand dollars. I had given the money to Freddy and told him to pass it on to Roche so that he could skip town. The heat was on, and every cop in the city was looking to find out who killed the boss. Springfield homicide detectives, The State Police, and the FBI were turning over every rock to find the killer. Roche had taken the money and disappeared. I later found out he fled to Florida.

That afternoon, the Bruno family had a gathering at their house, and I attended, even though I orchestrated his murder. At the time, nobody had any inclination that I had anything to do with the shooting. I moved around the house, acting surprised just like everyone else, offering my sincere condolences.

I had a conversation with Depergola, and he asked me if he should cooperate with the authorities because he saw the face of the shooter. I told him to consider that whoever shot Bruno was still on the loose, and if he had the balls to shoot a Made guy, killing a witness wouldn't matter to him. I also told him that we would find the killer and take our revenge for Bruno and his family.

The word on the street was that Roche killed Bruno because he thought Bruno was going after him for the bar-trashing incident. I had a conversation with Bruno's son Victor, and I told him that Roche had disappeared, and as I suspected, this was leaked to the press and law enforcement. Now, everyone was thinking that Roche was dead, and that was my plan to take the heat off us. The news media reported that Roche was probably killed in retaliation for shooting the boss.

Freddy, Ty, and I had a conversation about Roche, and we concluded that he was a risk to us, and he had to be killed.

I met with Artie, and he agreed that Roche was a loose end and he had to go. Artie said we needed to send a message that nobody kills a Made guy and walks away. He also said we should leave Roche's body on the street with both hands cut off and placed on his chest. This is a sign that the hand that pulls a trigger to kill a Made guy will end up being cut off. I agreed, and now we had to put together a plan to get to Roche.

Freddy contacted Roche and asked for a meeting to talk about how he would be working with our crew and how we would make a lot of money together. We met at a restaurant in Springfield, but Roche came with a couple of other people, so we couldn't get to him. He appeared to be nervous and extremely cautious. We tried meeting with him again, asking him to come alone to talk business confidentially. Once again, he came with his girlfriend and another guy.

Soon after we met with Roche, Freddy and Ty were arrested for assault and battery with a baseball bat. I was under indictment and out on bail; the cops had me under surveillance and had bugged just about every place I went. It would be way too risky for me to go after Roche *now*.

Nine months after killing Bruno, Roche was arrested in Tampa, and during the arrest, he was accidentally shot by an FBI agent. In December 2005, Roche was charged with the murder of Al Bruno. The day before he went to trial, he gave a statement implicating Freddy in the murder, and Freddy was arrested in Florida for first-degree murder. This was the beginning of a federal, state, and local investigation into who was involved in the hit on Bruno and why.

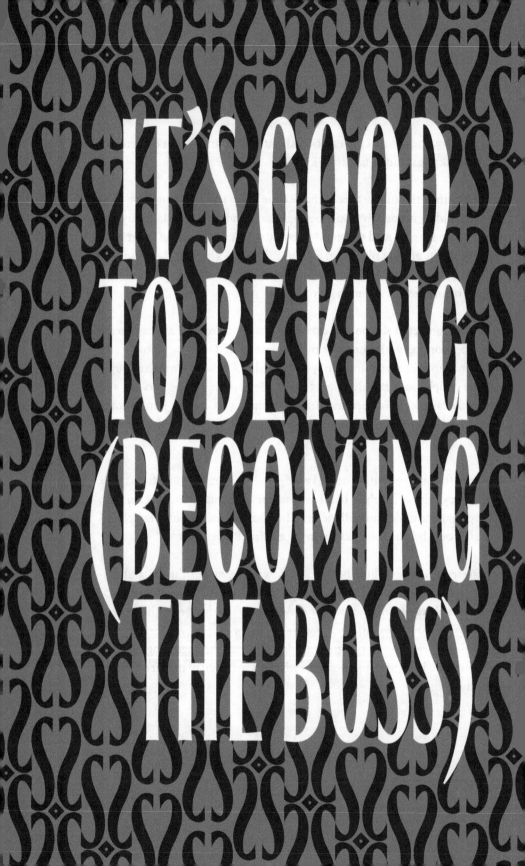

IT'S GOOD TO BE KING (BECOMING THE BOSS)

CHAPTER 17

When I talk about being the boss, I'm referring to being a captain in charge of our area. The actual boss of the Genovese family is always based out of New York. When I took over for Bruno there were three guys calling the shots for the Genovese family. At the time, the Genovese family was considered the most powerful of all New York families. Over the years, our family moved into many profitable legitimate businesses. We were involved in sanitation, unions, entertainment, construction, bars, restaurants, and the import-export business—to name a few.

The Genoveses have always been a very secretive family, and this may attest to why they are the strongest criminal organization today. In many cases, they would have a face known as the boss on the street, but the real boss was hidden behind the scenes.

This was the case with me. As Bruno was beginning to fall apart, I was told by the New York bosses that I was the guy in charge, but I needed to keep it confidential. They thought it would be wise to sacrifice a guy like Bruno, who they considered a risk to the family, and keep a trusted guy like me in control.

Soon after Bruno was killed, I took over his business operations. I assumed the numbers business, loan-sharking, extortion, and sports gambling. I also took over a couple of bars and restaurants where Bruno was a partner. I was still moving large quantities of pot and coke on the side, and I also moved into the vending-machine business. I was extremely busy with all the new ventures I had taken on, and at the same time, I was under deep surveillance by the FBI and the State Police. I figured I was being bugged and had to watch out for snitches. In addition, a court order was in place that kept me under a curfew from six in the evening to six in the morning—I had to be at home.

With all this going on, I still made sure I lived a good life. I would go out for an early dinner every night at the best restaurants, and I'd drink expensive wines and scotches, finishing the day with a nice cigar and high-end cognac. After arriving back at the house, I'd hold meetings with my crew, but they would have to sneak in through the back because the FBI would often be parked on the street. The women were plentiful, and they would come and go as I moved from one to another with an immense appetite—I was in my mid-thirties.

It was around this time that I found out who had shot up my house. Anthony Capua was the trigger man, and he had gotten the order from Tony Manzi out of Italy. I wanted to kill Capua so badly I could taste it, but I knew it was too risky with the feds tailing me, so I decided that could wait for now. My disappointment with Tony was beyond words because I thought we had a solid friendship and he had pleaded with me over the phone denying that he had anything to do with the shooting. He was now a proven liar and could never be trusted again. If he ever returned to the States, I'd have a big surprise waiting for him.

Unfortunately, soon after I learned that Capua was the shooter, he was arrested for drug trafficking and was facing serious time. I would have to get to him on the inside, which could be costly in more ways than one.

▼ ▼ ▼

After speaking with Artie Nigro, we decided it was time for me to take over the vending-machine business in the Springfield area. This was a huge moneymaker, bringing in hundreds of thousands a month. The biggest cash cow was the Joker Poker machines. These gaming machines were paying out in cash, and people were waiting in line to try their luck at bars, restaurants, clubs, and bodegas. Bartenders would manage the cash flow, and we would go in weekly to collect. We had other gaming machines, snacks, and cigarette machines, and the quarters and bills added up quickly.

Michael Cimmino controlled most of the vending machines in the area under the name S&M Vending Company. Now that I had the power and was backed by the New York guys, people feared me. There was also a whisper on the street that I was responsible for murdering people. I set up a meeting with Cimmino at my house and told him that I was taking over the vending machines and that he had to take his machines out of all the bars so I could install mine. He pleaded with me not to cut him out and he began whining. After speaking with Baba, I made an offer to buy S&M Vending company, and we agreed on a price of nine hundred thousand dollars. Very seldom do I like to use my own money to purchase businesses, so I engaged with Jimmy Santaniello, and he put up the cash. Once we were up and running, Cimmino came crying to me again, and I decided to let him keep some of his machines at our client's establishments. The deal was he would give me a cut off all his machines in operation, and he agreed.

Carlo Sarno also had a vending machine company, and he would service towns surrounding the city. He had a few machines in Springfield, but we had the lion's share. I would have squeezed him out of business, but he was a Made guy and was related to Mario Fiore.

I arranged a sit-down with Jerry Sarno and Mario Fiore. At that meeting, I told them I wanted them to remove their machines out of forty-five establishments and that I would move mine in. That didn't go over well.

After haggling back and forth, we agreed that they would keep their machines, but they were to pay me fifteen hundred a month, and they agreed. I always go in hitting hard, knowing they will offer me a good taste of the operation in the end. *Aim for the clouds and you'll probably end up on a mountain. Aim for a mountain and you'll end up on a small hill.*

There was one other player in the vending machine business in our area, Emilio "Emo" Gonzales. I met with him and told him he was to give me a piece of his earnings, and when he declined, I threatened his life. What I didn't know was that he was a federal informant, and he came to the meeting wearing a wire. I was arrested for extortion, but I ended up beating the case in court.

I was the boss of Springfield, Hartford, Albany, and part of New Haven. I was traveling to Boston, Worcester, and New Haven to meet with other Made guys to brainstorm how we could make money together. I met with Carmen "The Cheese Man" DiNunzio in Boston. Carmen was a huge guy who weighed in at over three hundred pounds. He earned his nickname because he owned and operated a fresh cheese shop in Boston's North End. Originally from Providence, Carmen was a Made guy with the Patriarca family. We met at a restaurant, where I watched him eat enough food to fill three guys. Carmen and I talked about working together in the sanitation business—there's big money in garbage. We ended up putting a deal together, and I made some good money in that sector.

I was always looking to find ways to make money, which is why I was considered the top earner in our area. This, combined with my willingness to do violence, was the reason I became a Made guy with the Genovese family. I was constantly thinking of ways to tap into various businesses and schemes to increase my cash flow. That's about the time I began thinking about the Grant brothers.

▼ ▼ ▼

Michael and Tony Grant had a string of businesses throughout Connecticut, Massachusetts, and New York, and they were also involved in selling drugs. The Grants were full-blooded Italian, but their father, William, had changed his name after arriving in the United States. He believed it would help him in the business world.

William "Hot Dog" Grant lived in East Hartford, where he owned Augie and Ray's hot dog restaurant. William was into a lot more than selling hot dogs. He was a high-level earner for the Patriarca family, where he ran a huge sports gambling operation bringing in millions of dollars a year. William was connected to many gangsters in all five New York families, and he spent

In court on a racketeering charge two days after the Bruno hit

a lot of time in New York hosting late-night parties. This helped him deepen his ties with the New York mobsters. One favor he did for the Colombo family, however, would cost him his life.

The notorious Carmine "The Snake" Persico's brother Alphonse was on the run from the feds. He fled his Brooklyn home in 1980 after being indicted on federal racketeering charges. Alphonse was a Made guy with the Colombo family, and they helped him hide out while he was on the lam. After moving around to various safe houses, William agreed to harbor Alphonse in Connecticut at the request of the Colombo family. Alphonse Persico was arrested in 1987 while hiding in a West Hartford apartment. At the pretrial discovery, it became known that William had disclosed to federal Marshals where Alphonse was staying. It was also believed that William had stolen a significant amount of money from Alphonse while he was on the run from the law.

The Colombo family boss sat down with the Genoveses, the Gambinos, and Billy "Wild Guy" Grasso to decide the fate of William Grant. He was a confirmed informant and turncoat. It was unanimous that William had to be taken out, and they determined the best person to do that was Grasso. Even though Grasso was William's mentor and partner, Grasso wanted to take over William's lucrative businesses. In Grasso's mind, there was no such thing as loyalty—it all came down to money, and this was the perfect opportunity to kill two birds with one stone.

On May 23, 1988, Grant disappeared on the way to his son's graduation party. His body was never found. Grasso had said that if he knew he was heading to his son's graduation, he would have delayed the hit until a week later. Grasso was now free to control William's businesses as he had always intended to.

I had known the Grant brothers since childhood because our families knew each other, and I always found them to be decent kids. Their father had left them a significant amount of money and some contacts in the business world, which helped get them started. They owned successful bars and restaurants and ran a widespread sportsbook. The brothers were also selling large quantities of coke and pot, and I approached them to do business.

Because I knew them, I asked them to front me around a quarter of a million in drugs, and I never paid them. I also beat them out of thousands in sports-betting debt.

The Grants bought a strip club in Manhattan called the Hustler Club, which was doing very well. Larry Flynt, the owner of *Hustler* magazine had a piece of the business for allowing them to use his brand.

I had a conversation with Artie, and we came to the agreement that the Grants were going to pay us twelve thousand a week for us to allow them to do business in New York. When I approached Michael Grant on the new deal, he wasn't very receptive. After that, Artie sent a dozen guys over to the Hustler Club, but the Grant brothers weren't there. And so the knockaround guys had a good time with the girls. They ran up a considerable bill drinking and eating, and before they left, they told the bartender to tell the Grants that their new partners, the Genoveses, came by to say hello. The bill was in the thousands, and they walked out without paying a dime.

I set up a meeting with Michael at the Hustler Club to go over his payment arrangements, and I intended to throw him a severe beating. Freddy and Ty came along, and they not only wanted to beat him, but they also wanted to maim him. After arriving, we concluded we wouldn't be able to throw him a beating because he had other people with him, and it was crowded. I also had a curfew and had to be home by six o'clock, and time was running out.

Michael was smart enough to not go outside to talk with us. I told him that we would kill him and his brother if he didn't start paying me twelve thousand a week. Looking into the crazed eyes of Ty Geas, Michael was clearly shaken up, and he agreed.

A few days went by, and I had a meeting with two captains in the Patriarca family. They warned me that the Grant brothers were federal rats and were talking with the FBI. They also told me that John Bologna was also a rat and that I should be cautious. The next day my attorney Vinny Bongiorni called me and told me that the FBI reached out to him to advise him that I was a target for investigation for extorting the Grant brothers. It turned out that the two Patriarca capos were right. Like father, like sons; the Grants were all rats. Vinny told me the only reason the feds would make such a call to him is to keep their informants safe. The Grants must have been giving them detailed information on other mobsters. Vinny advised me to back off and stay clear of the Grants. Reluctantly, I followed his advice.

In 2010, I was arrested and charged with extorting the Grants plus first-degree murder, racketeering, money laundering, loan-sharking, and inter-state commerce.

FULL OF
BOLOGNA

CHAPTER 18

The common denominator for the demise of the Springfield Crew is John Bologna. He was primarily responsible for causing dissension between the New York and Springfield factions of the Genovese family. Bologna played a key role in orchestrating the murder of Bruno and the attempted murder of Dadabo, as well as the contemplated hits on Louie Santos and Mario Fiore. He was steering the ship that ultimately sank the Springfield Crew.

John Bologna was born in Yorktown, New York, and was raised in Port Chester, a nearby community. His reign as a connected mobster started in 1966 when he began working off a debt for a local loan shark who he owed money to. This gave him momentum to break into low-level gambling operations with the Gambino family. The Gambinos also had a big stake in the trash removal businesses in the New York area, and Bologna became involved in the day-to-day operation of the garbage business.

During this time in the 1960s and 1970s, Bologna was arrested on several occasions for illegal gambling, which ultimately landed him in prison.

Bologna was a large, bearded guy standing over six feet tall and weighing over two hundred and fifty pounds. He was known for wearing Hawaiian type floral shirts and smoking big cigars. Bologna used to boast about his connections with famous people like John Gotti, Sammy Gravano, Madonna, Donald Trump, and other New York businessmen.

While working with the Gambinos, Bologna started running his own small crew conducting gaming and loan-sharking operations. Eventually he was operating out of a social club near Port Chester where he ran high-stakes card games and hosted Cosa Nostra meetings.

In 1999, Bologna switched alliances from the Gambinos and began working for the Genovese family—he was considered a puddle jumper.

During his affiliation with the Gambino family, Bologna was approached by federal agents who eventually turned him, and he became an informant. This was the beginning of a long and tumultuous relationship with the FBI that continued while he worked for the Genovese family, and right up to his imprisonment.

In the mid-1990s FBI records showed that Bologna began meeting with Special Agent Robert Bukowski on a regular basis providing information on the New York families. He was filtering information on individual mobsters, who were connected guys and Made members. Bologna gave detailed information on gambling and loan-sharking operations as well as corrupt unions, stolen-car operations, and the very lucrative trash-removal business.

Even though Bologna had begun working for the Genovese family, he kept close ties with some of the Gambino crew. This allowed him the opportunity to continue feeding his handler information that wouldn't directly impact his current situation with the Genoveses.

He funneled information to Bukowski regarding the changes that were taking place after John Gotti was arrested for the murder of Paul Castellano and other mobsters. The FBI was very interested in who took over the family after Gotti was behind bars and Bologna was keeping them informed. He told them the four new captains of the Gambino family had no confidence in John Gotti Jr., and they were thinking about replacing him because he didn't have the experience and intelligence to run the family. This was important information for the FBI because there was turmoil in the family with the removal of the former captains and the replacements who were now the shot-callers.

Even though Gotti Jr. was tried in federal court four times, he wasn't convicted. Elie Honig was the U.S. Attorney on the case against the junior Gotti, and he had given up on going after Gotti after his last trial in 2010. Honig went on to lead the first Bruno trial in 2011.

Bologna was a shifty, manipulating guy who carried a big personality that allowed him to rub elbows with many different wiseguys throughout the five families plus some politicians and celebrities.

On many occasions Bologna ordered his crew to administer beatings, commit arson, and threaten anyone who tried to stand in his way. He used to brag that he was asked to become a Made guy, but he declined stating, "I'm better than Made guys." His rationale was that Made guys had targets on their backs by the Feds and he stayed clear of that by remaining an associate—which was clearly a lie.

According to FBI reports, Bologna provided information on local politicians, State's Attorneys, and New York elites including Donald Trump who were hobnobbing with well-known Mafia members and associates.

In 2002, Bologna began funneling information to his FBI handler about the Springfield Crew. They documented that there were six Made members of the Springfield Crew at the time including Bruno, Delevo, Tranghese, and Baba Scibelli. Bologna couldn't name the other two members.

As Bologna worked his way deeper into the New York Genovese family, he was spending a lot of time around Artie Nigro—he was kissing Nigro's ass. Nigro asked him to be his driver, which he did for quite a while.

After being Nigro's driver he was moved up to taking on certain tasks. Nigro ordered Bologna to go up to Springfield on a weekly basis and get a clear understanding of business operations and the amount of cash that was flowing through the hands of their northern friends.

John
Bologna

Bologna was traveling to Springfield on weekends as Nigro's spy, and he used to frequent the Mardi Gras strip club like a kid in a candy store. He would sit in the corner with a drink and a cigar and count the number of customers that came in. Then he would calculate an average on what the cover charge and bar spending would come to in a day. Bologna would also pick connected guys' brains to get a clearer understanding of other business operations throughout the city and he would report back to Nigro.

After watching the Springfield operation for a while, Bologna told Nigro that Springfield was a cash cow, and they should be heavily taxed. The consensus was that Springfield was just an arm of the New York family, and they hadn't been kicking anything down to New York, and that had to change.

Nigro ordered Bologna to begin putting pressure on Springfield businesses to begin kicking money down to the New York bosses. It started with Bologna telling Jimmy Santaniello, the owner of the Mardi Gras, to pay a monthly fee to New York. When Bruno found out about the extortion of Santaniello, he told him to ignore Bologna and to pay him the money instead, and that he would work it out with New York.

When Bologna told Nigro that Bruno was stopping businesses from paying him, he was livid. He also told Nigro that Bruno was bad-mouthing him, stating Nigro had no stake in the money being earned in Springfield.

While Bologna was stirring the pot of resentment and anger between Nigro and Bruno, he was collecting money from the FBI as their informant. He was enjoying free meals, drinks, and access to the strippers while extorting businesses and filling his pockets any way he could. Bologna was taking in thousands from Springfield businesses and gambling operations while he was spying for Nigro.

As tensions increased, Patsy "Scop" DeLuca, a captain from the New York family, came to Springfield to look around, and at the same time, induct a couple guys into the family. Eugene "Rooster" Onofrio, who now allegedly runs the New Haven area, and Tony Volpe both became Made guys.

When DeLuca reported his findings back to Nigro, it was confirmed that Springfield boss Al Bruno was holding out on them, and he had to be dealt with. This would be the final hit that Bologna would be involved in directing.

Not only was Bologna good at creating tension between New York and Springfield, he was involved in the plotting of murders of wiseguys on both sides of the family. He was nudging Nigro to kill Santos and Fiore, which never happened. Bologna provided weapons to do violence and he sold two AK-47s to me, and one was used by Frankie Roche to shoot at Manzi in downtown Springfield.

Bologna was the instigator for most of the tension that arose in Springfield right up to the Bruno murder. When Bologna came to Springfield, it was as though dollar signs flashed before his eyes, and he saw a city that was ripe for the taking. He was always pitting mobsters against each other and creating strife where none had previously existed—he was toxic.

After I was inducted into the family, Nigro had a plan to demote Bruno back to soldier status, and I would take control as boss of the Springfield area.

The plan to demote Bruno came to an end when it became known he was working with the feds. As soon as Nigro learned about this, he ordered a hit on Bruno. Once again, Bologna was behind the plotting to kill another mobster, but this time it was a captain, and this one wouldn't fail.

After Bruno was killed and I took over as boss of the area, rumors on the streets had me responsible for the disappearance of Westerman and the Bruno murder—I had solid street credibility. No former captain from our area had these accolades, and this put me at a whole new level.

For seven years, I ruled the streets from Springfield to Albany and northern Connecticut. When things heated up over the Bruno hit, I was approached by Bologna who was trying to get me to talk about the murder. I had a bad feeling about him in my gut and I didn't tell him anything—I played dumb. It turned out that he was wearing a wire that day.

After the arrests for the Bruno murder, Bologna was never asked to testify at trial because the federal prosecutor said he was too untrustworthy and held back tons of information over the years. He was deemed an unreliable witness—a liar.

At the trial, I testified against Bologna, and it didn't bother me one bit. If it weren't for Bologna, things probably would have taken a different course, a better course. In the end, I was Bologna's undoing. He died in prison of prostate cancer in 2013—he was seventy-five.

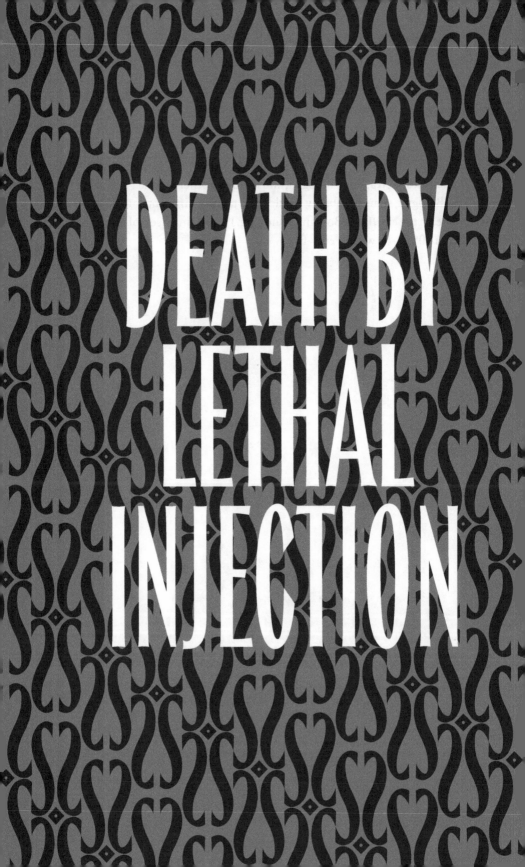

CHAPTER 19

I was drinking with my friend Bobby Spano at the Dante Club in West Springfield when he received a phone call. After talking for a minute, he turned to me and said that bookmaker John "Johnny Meatballs" Piteo was on the phone and he's saying that John Bologna was taken off the street by U.S. Marshals.

"Hello," I said wondering if this was true, and hoping it wasn't.

"Hey, it's John."

"Yeah, what's going on?"

"I just heard that John Bologna was taken into the federal witness protection program."

"What! Who told you this?" I felt a warm, ominous feeling rush through my body. I knew this was a real problem if it were true.

"I can't say right now. I can meet with you if you want."

"Yeah, we should talk in person. I'll call you back."

"Okay, I'll wait to hear from you." The line went dead.

I handed the phone back to Bobby. A weird feeling began growing in the pit of my stomach. I tried to drown it with a strong cognac, and I said good-bye to Bobby and left.

I met with my attorney Vinny Bongiorni at his office and told him about Bologna. He asked me what Bologna had on me? I told him he had every-thing on me, and he could bury me. Vinny said we should not panic and wait and see what happens.

I was expecting to be arrested at any moment. I found myself looking over my shoulder whenever I left the house; I was a bit paranoid. I told my wife and girlfriend that I might be arrested at any time, and they were both very supportive.

A few days passed, and I got a call from Freddy, who was being held for the murder of Bruno. He had been picked up in Florida after Roche gave a state-ment implicating him in the assassination. Freddy told me that FBI agents went to see his attorney and wanted him to convince Freddy and Ty to coop-erate in the murder investigation. He was also told that the case was being moved to the Southern District of New York. Both Freddy and Ty refused to cooperate with the FBI, and at this point, I started to get my affairs in order.

I went to see Emilio Fusco and I let him know that indictments for the Bruno murder would likely be coming down soon. I asked him to help me get a hundred-and-fifty thousand in the form of a check. Vinny didn't want to represent me in the Bruno case because they had been friends, but he recommended John Mitchell, who used to be John Gotti's attorney. I had the cash, but Mitchell needed payment in the form of a check. Refusing to help me confirmed that Fusco was one of the stupidest people on earth. He was involved in the murder of Bruno and Westerman, and one would think he would bend over backward to help me avoid being taken down. I never ended up retaining Mitchell as my attorney because once I decided to coop-erate I retained a different lawyer who had experience with clients who were turning state's evidence.

A month had passed since we received the call from Piteo. I was half asleep in my living room when I heard cars pulling up outside. I looked at the

clock, and it was a little before five in the morning, so I peeked out the window and saw a small army of law enforcement officers walking towards my house—I opened the door. FBI Agents, State Police, and Springfield Police had come to take me away, and I was informed that I was under arrest for the murder of Al Bruno. They were very polite and respectful, not to wake my family, and they told me I could get dressed. They waited until I was about to be placed into a cruiser before they cuffed me. As I sat in the back seat of the police car, I looked at my house and saw my family standing on the front steps watching me being carted away on a murder charge. My heart sank.

State Police Detective Tom Murphy was heading up the organized crime task force, which had been investigating me for years. Murphy was always professional and a gentleman, and he treated me respectfully. Detectives Murphy and Mike Imelio took me to a building on Main Street, where they told me Artie was listed as first on the inditement, and I was listed as second. At that point, Artie was doing time and would be released soon. Murphy suggested that Artie would probably cooperate to avoid spending the rest of his life in prison. I knew Artie was a bigger prize for the feds than I was. After all, he was a boss of the biggest Mafia family in the country. Murphy said I should consider cooperating before Artie did, but I refused.

Federal Marshals took control of me and took me to the federal building lock-up. I woke up the following day in a cell, thinking that the night before, I was lying on the couch with my two little girls holding them close. Less than thirty-six hours later, I'm sitting in a shithole waiting to be processed for murder. A bit of depression was trying to take hold—I fought it.

That same day, I was in a courtroom before a judge, and I pleaded not guilty. The judge asked the prosecutor what the recommended penalty was, and the prosecutor replied, "Death by lethal injection." I knew I couldn't show it, but my heart felt like it dropped and landed in my shoe.

CHAPTER 20

I was transferred to Wyatt Detention Facility in Rhode Island, where I was immediately put into solitary confinement, and I rotted in that cell for a week. This was a high-profile murder case, and they didn't want to take any chances with me ending up murdered or killing another inmate. I was also considered a suicide risk, but that never crossed my mind.

Before I had changed lawyers, Attorney John Mitchell visited me and told me he spoke with Ernie Muscarella, a Genovese boss. He said that Ernie told him that the New York guys were nervous because Artie was no longer in the system, and he must have been moved. Ernie and the other top wise-guys were thinking that Artie had flipped. We discussed the case in detail, and after he left I thought hard about what Murphy had said—Artie would probably turn state's evidence to avoid a life sentence.

My girlfriend Michelle came to see me, and soon after, my wife and kids visited. Seeing them is what helped me to keep going and maintain my sanity. I had a lot to think about because I knew that in the end, it's really all about family.

A few days later, Vinny came to visit.

"How are you holding up, Anthony?" He was dressed in an expensive Italian-made suit. Me, not so much.

"How do you think? I feel like shit!"

"I understand," he said with a look of compassion. "You need to know that Fusco and Tranghese are being served subpoenas on your case."

"Do you think they'll talk?"

"Word in the courthouse is that Fusco is going to refuse to talk, but that Tranghese is going to cooperate."

"That doesn't surprise me, he's always been an untrustworthy shithead."

"What are your thoughts on this new information?"

"Vinny, all of this is stacking up against me now, and I'm going to be drowning in a pile of shit," I said. "They have Roche, Bologna, Felix, and most likely Artie, and they are all preparing to spill their guts. You don't have to be a rocket scientist to figure out who they're going to point their fingers at." I looked Vinny in the eye and said, "I'm never going to get out."

He nodded his head. "Again, what do you want to do?" He knocked on the table three times. "I suggest a preemptive strike."

I sat in silence processing what was now in front of me. "Yeah, we should strike first before it's too late," I said.

"You know they'll want to talk about bodies."

"I understand." I knew he meant they would want statements regarding murder, not just racketeering.

"Okay, let me feel out the U.S. Attorney and I'll get back to you."

"Thanks, Vinny. I really appreciate you." I shook his hand, and he was off. I knew he wasn't going to directly represent me and he was acting as an advisor and a friend and I appreciated it.

That day I told my wife Irene I was thinking of cooperating, and I wanted to get her thoughts on it. This was a life-changing decision, and I needed to know where she stood. I told her if I went into the witness-protection program, we could move and start over, and things would work out fine. She agreed without hesitation.

I asked Irene to reach out to Nicki Geas, Freddy and Ty's cousin, to ask her to come and visit me. I needed her to get a message to the brothers that I was going to cooperate. And that I wanted them to get on board with me to make a deal to save our ass—a preemptive strike. She said she would take care of it.

My girlfriend came to visit, and she agreed I should cooperate. Michelle was worried that I was facing life in prison, and maybe death if I didn't. At that point, I was steadfast in my decision to move forward with providing state's evidence.

I was waiting to hear from Vinny on what the U.S. Attorney was thinking regarding my decision to talk, but Vinny wasn't getting back to me. Then I got word that his father suddenly passed away, and when I finally spoke with him, he said he needed time to grieve.

To make things worse, when I called Michelle to tell her about Vinny's father dying, she told me she couldn't talk because she was on the other line with my wife Irene. She said Irene found out about our affair and was upset and bawling over the phone. This was all I needed at this point. What else was going to go wrong now? I told her I would call Irene and work it out. She wasn't optimistic.

The conversation with Irene didn't go well. I tried telling her that I loved her and that I had made a bad mistake. I told her that she and the kids were all that mattered to me, that I would stop seeing Michelle, and I would make it up to her. It fell on deaf ears. I asked her if she had spoken to Nicki about coming to see me. She said she was going too, but now that was off the table. There would be no forgiveness—I had betrayed her.

From that point on, my primary conduit to the outside world was shut down. I wasn't getting any messages from Vinny or our friends—she completely shut me out.

Felix Tranghese,
Dora Scibelli, and
Baba Scibelli

Finally, Vinny came to see me, bringing Tom Butters, an attorney from Boston along with him. Butters said he would work with the U.S. Attorney to try and get me a deal if I decided to retain him for the case I trusted Vinny and agreed to hire Tom as my attorney. I told him to disclose that I would talk about the Bruno murder and other shootings they would be interested in. He left with a bandolier full of ammunition. A few days later, Butters returned and said the U.S. Attorney was interested in making a deal.

I was relocated to MDC in Brooklyn for a few days and then again to MCC in New York City. After arriving, they stuck me in solitary for three days and it seemed like an eternity before moving me to a cell. I figured they were preparing me to go to court to meet with the U.S. Attorney, and I was right. The next day, I was transported to the federal courthouse, where the federal prosecutor's office was located. I was taken to a conference room where Butters was waiting to meet with me. I had a funny feeling about my new attorney, but I couldn't put my finger on it.

There were around fifteen people inside the room, including the Prosecutor, FBI Agents, and State Police from Massachusetts, New York, and Connecticut. They began asking me a bunch of questions. I would answer, and they would leave the room for a huddle, then return and start again. After several times, I told Butters I needed to make a phone call—I was becoming apprehensive about turning. I called Irene and Michelle, and they both said I should go forward and cooperate. I told my lawyer to offer a plea deal to the prosecutor that I would cooperate for a fifteen-year sentence. I figured with good behavior I could be out in a little over twelve years. The answer was no.

At that point, I had to shit or get off the pot, so I sucked it up and began talking. I told them about Bologna being at the center of everything bad that had happened and how he was involved in setting up the hit on Dadabo in New York. It turned out they had no idea I was involved in the shooting of the cement-union steward.

They left the room again to discuss the new information. When they returned, they asked me about how I became a Made guy, and I told them the story. They asked about Gary Westerman, and I gave them everything on the hit. They asked if I could show them where the body was buried, and I said I knew exactly where his gravesite was. We talked about the Bruno killing and who was involved in planning that out. One of the Connecticut investigators asked me if I killed Joe Mazzotta in Connecticut. I knew that Mazzotta was a Mob-connected murder, but I had nothing to do with it—I said no.

After another huddle, they returned to the room and agreed to make a deal with me. The next day, I was arraigned for murder, and I pleaded not guilty. To my surprise, Artie was in court and was also arraigned. He was at MDC the whole time and hadn't cooperated with authorities, and he didn't know that I had turned state's evidence.

He was sitting next to me, and he leaned in close to my ear. "Can you believe that scumbag, Bologna? Fucking rat," Artie wisped.

"Everyone told you he was a rat, but you didn't listen," I said.

He looked at me and nodded in disgust. I'm sure the conversation would have gone differently if he had known I was also cooperating.

I signed the agreement the next day and was shipped to Westchester County Department of Corrections. Two weeks later, I was transported to my old safe-house property in Agawam, where I showed the authorities where Westerman's remains were buried, and they dug him up.

It took over a year for the trial to commence, and I had to testify in open court against my old friends, Freddy, Ty, and Artie. Felix also testified in open court, and Fusco had escaped to Italy, but was arrested and extradited to the States a couple of months later. He ended up getting twenty-five years in prison. Freddy and Ty refused to cooperate—they were thickheaded and believed that cooperating with law enforcement would label them as rats and for them there was nothing worse.

The bottom line is that I had to think of my family when cooperating. Every one of the guys I testified against would have killed me in a second if it was in their best interest. My family is the only thing I truly cared about. They had to come first.

CHAPTER 21

When most people think of prison, they believe it to be a horrific and dangerous place void of excitement and joy. In many cases, this may be true; but it wasn't my experience. During my time behind bars, I met some of the most interesting and cunning people I have ever encountered.

In prison you can get drugs, liquor, good food, and in some cases, women. I was in the best physical shape of my life while I was inside, working out every day. Inmates can count on three meals a day, and most have no stressful responsibilities to burden them. Now, I can truly understand how some people can become institutionalized. Don't get me wrong; I would much rather be living on the outside, but it wasn't as bad as I thought it would be before I was first sent away.

The first time I was sentenced to prison, I was transported to Concord State Penitentiary for four months, before being transferred to Gardner State Penitentiary for another eight months. I was convicted in 1990 for shooting a firearm out of a moving vehicle, possessing an illegal handgun without a permit, and violating probation.

Concord is a large facility located outside of Boston. It was rated as a level-four security prison that houses just under fourteen hundred inmates. It opened in 1878 and is the oldest operating prison in Massachusetts; and from its appearance, there's no denying that fact. Escaping from Concord is an extremely difficult feat because it is surrounded by a forty-foot concrete wall.

After being processed, I was moved to J Block (this is where they house the most violent criminals.) Two guys came to my cell and asked if I was Anthony Arillotta—I said yes. They said Ronnie Cassesso sent them, and they gave me a bag of food and assorted bathroom items. We talked for a minute, and I asked them if they knew Peter Limone, who was friends with our Springfield Crew, and they said they knew of him. At that point, they probably figured I was well-connected. The next day, I was moved to the East-Down building. That's where most of the Italian and Irish guys were staying.

Peter "Crazy Horse" Limone headed up the Boston branch of the Patriarca family. He was famous for beating a murder rap and was ultimately awarded a twenty-six-million-dollar money judgment in a case against the federal government for wrongful imprisonment. Limone and three other guys were arrested and charged with the gangland slaying of Irish gangster Teddy Deegan. The conviction was based on testimony from Patriarca enforcer Joe "The Animal" Barboza, who was later deemed to be an unreliable witness—he lied.

After being betrayed by the Patriarcas, Barbosa was flipped by the FBI, and he became a federal informant. When he finished testifying, he and his family were moved to California under the federal witness relocation program, and they were given new identities. Barbosa had assumed the new identity of Joe Denati, and he made the fatal mistake of reaching out to an old, connected friend James Chalmas while he was living out west. Chalmas set up Barbosa who was famously shotgunned to death by J. R. Russo in San Fransisco in 1976.

▼ ▼ ▼

Ronnie "The Pig" Cassesso was also incarcerated for the murder of Deegan, and he died in prison shortly after I was settled in. Limone and Cassesso were like kings at Concord, and they took me under their wing.

When I found out that Aniello Caracciolo had arrived, I asked that he be moved in with me. I had my own cell, and the Caracciolos were friends of my family, and I knew him. Aniello was given a six- to nine-year manslaughter sentence for killing a guy in a bar fight. He was connected to the Patriarcas, and he worked under Gaetano Milano—the Made guy who killed Billy Grasso. Aniello was a good guy, and we got along well.

Concord had some good things going for it and some not-so-good. The facility had a decent gym, a big yard for working out with weights, a running track, a baseball diamond, a football field, and basketball courts. We were allowed to have a TV in our cell, and we had hot pots and microwaves to cook our own food. Unfortunately, the cafeteria food was terrible. The corrections officers were pricks, but there were a few who would look the other way when we were in violation of the rules. Drugs—mostly coke, pot, and heroin—were plentiful on the inside. It came in through corrupt guards and was snuck in by visitors. We were also able to get alcohol, both from the outside and hooch we distilled ourselves. When Christmas packages arrived, the soda inside the bottles were replaced with whiskey. Inmates were allowed three weekly visits for a couple of hours, and visitors would bring drugs in, hidden inside electronic appliances like TVs and microwaves. I never took drugs, but there was money to be made on the inside from drug sales.

When it came to sex, there were no conjugal visits at Concord. A few guys were lucky enough to get laid by female guards or counselors. Other than that, unless someone was okay with queers, we didn't have sex.

Just to be clear, Concord could be a dangerous place. Many inmates had homemade weapons, such as shivs for stabbing and razors taped to toothbrushes for slicing. The guards would have random shakedowns from time to time, so we had to be careful not to get caught with a weapon. That would get you time in the hole, and days spent in solitary confinement seemed to drag on forever.

Most of the gangs inside were Latin Kings and Bloods; however, there were some smaller gangs that clung together. Most of the white guys stuck together, and there were a lot of us. Doing time in Concord could be some real hard time for certain cons who were victims of beatings and stabbings—such as rival gang members, guys deemed rats or pedophiles, and cons who the guards had it in for. Nearly everyone could be at risk, and we always had to watch each other's back.

After the four months at Concord, I was moved to Gardner Correctional Institute in Massachusetts. This was a medium-security facility, and the COs were a little better in how they treated inmates.

Just as it was at Concord, we could wear street clothes, and the ability to get drugs, booze, and women were about the same. The difference at Gardner was that there weren't any cells in our building. Instead, it was an open bay with around forty inmates in each room. Bunk beds were lined up, and there were two floors where inmates slept. The basement was where the showers and recreation room were located. The complex had six buildings in operation, and we were able to roam to other buildings—depending on the guard on duty. They had a massive hangar with an area for weight training, and a heavy bag was hanging for us to pound out our frustrations. We played baseball, basketball, soccer, street hockey, and handball in the yard. The food at Gardner was much better than at Concord, and we could also cook our own food. Once a week, we went to the commissary, where we could buy up to fifty dollars in goods—that was the max. We were allowed four visits a week for four to eight hours a visit, and I looked forward to those visits. It wasn't too bad at Gardner as far as state prisons go because we had reasonable freedom to move around the facility and the staff wasn't overbearing.

The day I met Brian Goodman was during a street hockey game in the yard. He had been moved to Gardner from Norfolk because he beat down another inmate with a pipe. Brian was a tough guy who grew up in South Boston, and he ended up on the wrong side of the law. He used to rob drug dealers and had a reputation on the street as a force to be reckoned with. Right off the bat, Brian and I hit it off. I was around eight years younger than he was, and he became a mentor to me. I put in a word with a guard and had Brian moved into G building, where I was housed. We started working out together in the weight area, and he mainly concentrated on doing calisthenics. I was more of a weightlifter, but he quickly began teaching me the benefits of using your own body to get into top shape.

Christmas in
the can

Not long after I arrived, Ty Geas had been moved to Gardner and was also into weight training. Brian tried to convince Ty to do our calisthenics workout, but he refused. Ty was a champion wrestler in high school, and after I told Brian about his achievements, he approached Ty and challenged him to a wrestling match. Keep in mind Brian is a big, solid, and tough guy with many street fights behind him. He once bit off a guy's nose during an altercation and spit it out. Brian told Ty that if Ty couldn't pin him, he would have to start doing his calisthenics workout. Ty agreed, and they went at it. They rolled around the ground for at least five minutes, and Ty couldn't pin him. The next day, Ty joined us for Brian's workout.

I was walking the yard with Brian on a warm, sunny day when this guy approached us. He was a short, Irish-looking guy with dead eyes, like a shark. Brian introduced him as Mike Flaherty, a guy from South Boston who he knew from the street. I shook his hand, and he moved on—walking away like he owned the prison.

"See that guy?" Brian said

"Yeah."

"You should be friendly with him and show respect but keep your distance."

"Okay, why is that?" I asked.

"He killed a bunch of people on the street. He was one of Whitey Bulger's guys. So, after being sentenced to prison for life, he was involved with setting up around seven people who were killed on the inside. He's a nutcase with nothing to lose. Be careful around that guy."

"Good to know," I said, thinking he looked like a guy who couldn't be trusted.

"The way he operates is, if he doesn't like how you look, or anything about you rubs him the wrong way, he spreads the word that you're a pedophile or a rat. He uses Bulger's name and says that he heard it to be true from Bulger himself. In one case he had gotten all the inmates on the tier to participate in the murder. Everyone had to stab the guy at least once; that way, they were all implicated, and no one would talk. In some cases, a guy would be stabbed forty times, and he wasn't even a rat or a pedophile to begin with," Brian said with a serious look.

"You don't want to get on his bad side."

"No, I wouldn't. The only way around it is to kill him first."

"Right, or just stay clear, and be friendly and respectful," Brian said.

Brian and I were watching *The Arsenio Hall Show*, and he was interviewing James Caan.

"When I get outta here, that's what I wanna to do," Brian said.

"You want to be a talk-show host?"

He laughed. "No. I want to be an actor."

"Really?" I figured it was a far-fetched dream.

"That's right. Look, guys like James Caan play guys like us in the movies. We're the real deal. So doesn't it make sense for us to play the part? It comes natural to us because it's who we are."

"True, but you still need to know how to act in front of a camera," I said.

"I'll learn how to do that. I'm going to Hollywood when I get out. That's what I want to do with my life."

"Good luck with that," I said, thinking he was full of shit.

Brian went on to become a well-known actor and a director in Hollywood. He acted in movies with Robert Redford, Ethan Hawke, Mark

Ruffalo, and James Gandolfini, to name a few. To this day, Brian is a solid friend of mine.

▼ ▼ ▼

The second time I was sentenced to prison was in 2005. I was convicted of racketeering, loan-sharking, extortion, and money-laundering. I got three and a half years—five months in Concord, and the rest back at Gardner. Things had changed in the fifteen years since I was locked up at Concord. There were a lot more gangs inside now. The same gangs as before were still there, but now there were cartel gang members, and those guys were crazy. The prison stabbings and beatings had increased, and because of this, so did the security. There were no televisions in our cells, no outside packages, and we had to wear prison clothes. The food still sucked. Concord was worse than it was the first time I was there, and I was happy when I was moved to Gardner.

After arriving at Gardner, I was met by my friend, Jimmy Rodwell, who was still there since I last saw him in 1990. Jimmy was a good guy who was doing life for murder. He gave me a package to get me started, and I was off to the races. Many of the faces I saw were guys I met in my last stint—they were embedded in Gardner.

It was still lights out at nine-thirty, and headcount was at seven in the morning. Street clothes were no longer an option and we didn't have as much freedom to roam the compound. The violence had increased due to a higher gang presence, but that didn't affect me. This time, I had a reputation as a capo with the Genovese crime family—this earned me instant respect.

The Latin Kings were a force to be reconned with, and they underestimated the fury the white guys could lay on them. We had a lot of Italian and Irish guys inside, and we stuck together.

In July of 2005, things came to a head, and we ended up in a rumble with the Kings. Guys on both sides were stabbed, sliced, and beaten, but I think we got the best of them—we were stronger. Inmates from both sides ended up in the hole for being involved in the melee, but I managed to avoid solitary confinement and I was relieved—I hated being in the hole.

My world came crumbling down in 2007. I got a call that my father was critically ill, so I petitioned to go and see him in the hospital, and it was granted. I was extremely close to my dad, and I was grateful that I was able to visit him at Mercy Hospital. I held his hand as he faded in and out. He was heavily medicated for pain relief, but he was still able to acknowledge that I was there with him. Sadly, this was our last time together. My father died the next day; he was sixty-six years old.

Even though I was in prison, I was making around a hundred thousand a month. Before I went away, I had set up and organized my crew, so the money would continue to roll in, and it would be business as usual. Ralphie Santaniello and Richie Valentini handled the numbers, loan-sharking, and sports betting. Ryan Fattini was in charge of the marijuana operation and my legitimate businesses, and John Rodier was collecting my vending machine money. I had arranged that the cash would be dropped off at my parent's store, my wife's place, and houses of friends I trusted. Rodier would occasionally visit me to keep me abreast of what was happening on the street, and I have to mention my Aunt Suzie who was a huge support at the time. The telephones in prison weren't secure, so we had to be careful how we communicated with the outside world, so in-person conversations were critical.

In 2007, I was indicted for extorting the Sarnos and their vending-machine company. But the Sarno brothers refused to testify when it came time for trial. In the end, I think they valued their lives more than their poker machines. As a result, I was found not guilty.

Around a year after my father died, Irene had found out about my girl-friend, and she went on a spending spree. My wife blew through a million and a half of my hard-earned dollars. That was the beginning of the end of our marriage.

The third and last time I was sent to prison was in 2010 for the Bruno and Westerman murders. I was also convicted of extortion, money-laundering, loan-sharking, racketeering, and interstate commerce. This time I wasn't going away on a state rap. I was sentenced to eight and a half years in federal prison. Because I was tried out of a New York federal court, I was sent to Westchester County Prison in New York, where I was housed for a year while appearing in court.

I had my own cell, and they didn't allow television sets or cooking devices. We had to wear orange jump-suit prison garb. Everyone on my tier was a hard-core criminal—mostly in for murder. It was a tightly controlled facility with very strict guards, but drugs were still getting in. Some inmates would cook up their own moonshine, but it was limited. There was a small gym for working out, but nothing like I was used to at Gardner. The big thing at Westchester was cell phones being smuggled in. If we got caught, we knew we were going to the shoe, but most inmates took that chance when they could. I was able to spend around eight hours a day on a cell phone.

I spent one month at MCC in New York while testifying in court, before being moved to my permanent housing for the remainder of my sentence. I can't reveal the location of the federal prison I was at because it could negatively affect high-profile inmates with whom I had become friendly with. The prison was a witness-protection-program unit in New Jersey—that's all I can disclose.

This prison hosted some of the world's most cruel and vicious killers. It was a level-five facility, and it was well-operated. The food was great, we had TVs in our large cells, and the facilities were top-notch. It had a nice gym area with free weights and weight machines, and the yard was vast, with many fields set up for playing sports. There was a very nice movie room where we would go to watch recent motion pictures. It was a very clean facility, and the guards weren't as bad as I was used to at the state level. We were allowed to wear street clothes provided there was no gang-related attire or colors. They ran a tight operation with no drugs, booze, or sexual activity.

After arriving, I was placed in a cell with Joe "Big Joey" Massino, the former boss of the Bonanno family in New York that the movie *Donny Brasco* was inspired by. Joe was a serious guy, but he was solid. We had our differences from time to time, but we always worked through them. He was in for two murders but had admitted to killing at least a dozen other people while working his way up the ranks of the notorious family. He ended up pleading guilty to fourteen murders and he turned state's evidence to avoid the death penalty. He was the first boss to turn on his own family. Six months after being there, Joe was moved out of my cell, and I ended up having my own space, and that was nice.

When we had free time, we could move around from cell to cell, and that's when I got to know many of the guys there. I met Pedro Flores, El Chapo's top cartel associate. I became friendly with Peter "Bud" Zuccaro, a Made guy with the Gambino family who was responsible for several murders. He used to say, "I never killed people for money; I killed them for principle." I spent time with Philly wiseguy Teddy DiPretoro, who, along with Rocco Marinucci, was responsible for killing mob boss Phillip "The Chicken Man" Testa as he stepped onto his front porch. Testa was blown to bits in 1981 by a nail bomb that was constructed with ten sticks of dynamite. Three years later, his son Salvatore "Salvie" Testa was ordered killed by Nicky Scarfo, and he was found shot to death in a candy store.

I also knew Najibullah Zazi, who plotted to bomb a New York City subway car. I had conversations with Kevin Roach, an Aryan Brotherhood leader who was in for murder, and he admitted to being involved in twenty-four murders while behind bars.

Finally, I became closest to one of the worst mass murderers in human history, David Headley, a Pakistan-American guy whose cell was located on my tier. David was responsible for helping to plan the 2008 attack in Mumbai, India, which killed one hundred and seventy-four people and wounded more than three hundred. Headley admitted he had conducted five spying missions before the bombing under the direction of the Pakistani (ISI) intelligence agency. He was also an informant for the DEA, and analysts suggest he was a double agent against the United States. David is a very intelligent and devoted Muslim with whom I became good friends. We used to joke around and read excerpts from philosophy books and discuss the meaning of life. It's hard to believe a guy as nice as David could have so much blood on his hands. The wretched things men are capable of will always astound me.

CHAPTER 22

When it comes to my marriage falling apart, I admit that it was my fault. It wasn't that I didn't love my wife—because I did. It was just that my lifestyle wasn't conducive to a trustworthy relationship. Being a wiseguy isn't always favorable to maintaining a healthy marriage. The money and power attracted many women; it's as simple as that. I will say I have a weakness when it comes to the ladies—I love them. In this regard, I have my regrets. I had a good wife and a beautiful family, and I blew it.

With my wife Irene, things began turning in the wrong direction in 2001. I went out almost every night and came home late—sometimes when the sun was rising. I wasn't spending much time with my family, and Irene was getting pretty pissed off. She often brought it to my attention, but I brushed it off. Eventually, things came to a head, and people got hurt.

I received a call from Anthony Scibelli, who said Irene was at The Fort restaurant with her girlfriend, and there were a couple of guys with them. One of the guys was John Walczak, who owned a cigar shop in West Springfield where I used to hang out with my crew. I would often go in to buy cigars and smoke with my friends, and I would talk with John a few times a week.

When I confronted Irene about being at The Fort with John, she said he helped her get her car jumped after the battery died. I found out they had

With Santos, my ex-wife Irene, and Bruno

been with each other on a few occasions, but John never bothered to mention this to me when I saw him at his shop. I found this to be concerning because a guy I see all the time never told me how he helped my wife jump-start her car. I was a little angry about the whole situation, and my mind was racing, visualizing John fucking my wife. It may have been my imagination running wild, but I couldn't let it go. I kept pushing Irene on the matter, and she kept denying that she did anything wrong; and finally, she left with my son to stay at her mother's house. When I approached her at her mother's house, and she said John was only a friend, and nothing happened—I didn't believe her. I suggested we go to the cigar shop and meet with John to straighten the situation out. Her mother was there and said she wanted to come along with us because she wanted to know if her daughter was truly innocent. Now, we were all heading out to the cigar shop to pay John a visit and I was seeing red. I wanted to hurt him badly. I called a few guys in my crew and asked that they drive down there too, just in case John had some friends at the shop.

Six of us showed up at the shop, and when I approached John, I reached out to shake his hand like I had done so many times in the past. As I took his hand with my right, I gave him a straight punch to the face with my left, and he fell backward. Then, I started punching and kicking him in a frenzy. I smashed the cash register over his head, grabbed a brick from behind the counter, and hit him with that. He fell to the ground, and I broke a wooden box of fine cigars over his head. When he got to his feet, he began to stumble out the door and was nearly struck by a car as he staggered across the busy street. Irene and her mother had run to a pizza shop across the street and called the cops. We decided it was time to leave and fled as the police car siren sounded through the hot, sticky air.

The next day, I was with Bruno and told I him what had happened. I said I had to slap a guy a couple of times because there was a question that he may have been inappropriate with my wife. He was okay with it until he found out it was John. A couple of days later, he called me to meet with him at his restaurant. After arriving at Cara Mia, Bruno got in my face and told me that the father of the guy I beat down was a friend of Baba's. He said I didn't just slap the guy around as I told him I did. He said the guy had taken forty stitches, a broken jaw, and three broken ribs and was admitted into the hospital. I snapped at Bruno and asked him what he would have done if it was his wife? He backed off.

The whole ordeal was still eating at my core, and even though I threw him a beating, I wasn't finished with him. I had to know the truth, so I got John to agree to a three-way call with Irene; otherwise, I told him I would kill him. I arranged for John to call her and not reveal that I was on the other line. I made him tell her, "Anthony doesn't know anything about what we did." I had to hear her reaction, and then I would know if they had sex or not. On the call, John did exactly what I told him to do, and her reaction was, "there is nothing for Anthony to know—we didn't do anything wrong." I hung up, feeling comfortable that nothing inappropriate had happened. It was good for John because I was planning to kill him if he fucked my wife. I suppose John was innocent of banging my wife and maybe he shouldn't have taken such a vicious beating, but he should have told me he was seeing her and that he helped her with her car issue. To this day, I'm not sure his intentions were anything other than trying to get into her pants—she is a beautiful woman.

With all that was happening, we felt Irene should move out, so I set her up with an apartment where she stayed for around four months. During the separation, I banged her sister Sandra a few times, but for the record she came on to me.

We ended up reconciling, and Irene and my son, Anthony Jr. moved back in. It wouldn't be for another nine years until things finally came to a head.

A few days before I was arrested for the Bruno murder, Irene found Michelle's number on my cell phone. I had made a late-night call, and she was investigating who I was calling. I was now in law enforcement's custody, and I called Michelle to say hello, and she told me she was on the other line with Irene. My head started spinning. Why were my wife and my girlfriend chatting over a phone call? Irene called Michelle's number, acted like she was my sister, and began asking all kinds of questions. After building a rapport over a long call, Irene learned Michelle was my girlfriend, and that's when Irene told her she was my wife. I told Michelle to hang up, and that I would call Irene and work it out. When I called her, she was livid, yelling at me.

"How could you do this to our family? I hate you, and I want a divorce."

The next time I spoke with her, she said she wanted to kill Michelle. After that, every call seemed different when I spoke with her. She went from wanting a divorce, to killing Michelle, to wanting to try and work things out. Irene was all over the place—she was confused and indecisive. I had Michelle call her and tell her that we never had sex but were just good friends, but I don't think Irene believed her.

Eventually, my wife stopped visiting me in prison, and we divorced a year and a half later. I had left her around a hundred thousand dollars, yet she told everyone I left her penniless. I'm sure she didn't tell her friends and family how she blew through a million and a half of my money while I sat in prison for my prior conviction.

After being inside for a while, I found out that she was seeing a guy who cut hair, and soon after, they ended up getting married. To this day, Irene still hates me and won't allow me to see my daughters. Maybe one day she will learn to forgive me. I'm happy that my girls are being raised in a good family setting with love and stability. I'm grateful for that.

A FAMILY
TRAGEDY

CHAPTER 23

There are many ways to test the loyalty of family and friends. I can tell you firsthand that being arrested for murder will reveal the true colors of those around you. Everyone handles a situation like this differently. Some will drop everything and do all they can to help you emotionally and financially. Others will completely detach themselves from you and act as if they never knew you. And there are those who will tell you they are here to support you, but when you need their help, they can't be counted on. Unfortunately, there are also those who completely turn against you. Not only are they absent after the arrest, but they also bad-mouth you on the street and wish you poorly. It's amazing how many friends you have when you're on top of the world, but when you're at the bottom, they're nowhere to be found.

Michelle was always there for me. As Irene completely withdrew, only having contempt flowing through her veins, Michelle never abandoned me. Even to this day, I'm good friends with her—she loved me through good and bad. I will always appreciate how she stood by me, and I treasure her friendship and loyalty.

My son was sixteen years old when I was sent away. Before I left, I told him he was the man of the house now and that he needed to step up and look after the family in my absence.

I remember him telling me about a school project he was doing in his social studies class on current affairs. They had to research local Mafia goodfellas, and I was the main topic of discussion. The other kids knew I was his father. They were impressed that Anthony had a father who was a local organized crime boss who was in prison for murdering the old boss, Al Bruno. It's incredible to me how teenage boys think. I could have been best-selling author James Patterson or Tesla founder Elon Musk and they would find a Mob killer like me more interesting. In any case, my son took it in stride and handled it well. I think many kids of famous parents don't see them in the same light as the public. To them, you are just mom or dad, and the novelty of who you are wears off rather quickly.

My oldest daughter Sofia was six when I was incarcerated for Bruno's murder. She didn't know why I was leaving; she thought I was going away to work again. She was distraught that I was going to be leaving for an extended period, and it broke my heart to see the sadness in her eyes. My youngest child Grace didn't understand anything that was happening, but when she asked me if I had a girlfriend, it took the wind out of my sails. It was apparent that Irene was filling her head with negativity toward me, and I had to lie and tell her Michelle was just a friend. I haven't seen my daughters in thirteen years and miss them every day.

When it came to my mother, it was just the status quo. She wasn't surprised by my charges and convictions. She told me it was inevitable that I would end up in prison or dead by the way I chose to live my life. Unlike my father, my mother never knew I had become a Made member of the Genovese family. She may have heard rumors on the street, but I never told her. From her perspective, I think it was very disappointing, but expected that I would end up in the situation I created.

My grandmother Rose, on my father's side, was somewhat in denial about what she had read in the papers or heard from people around her. She was very religious, and I knew she was very upset about the entire ordeal. Rose used to ask me if what she heard was true, and I couldn't find it in my heart to hurt her, so I lied and told her it wasn't. She ended by stating

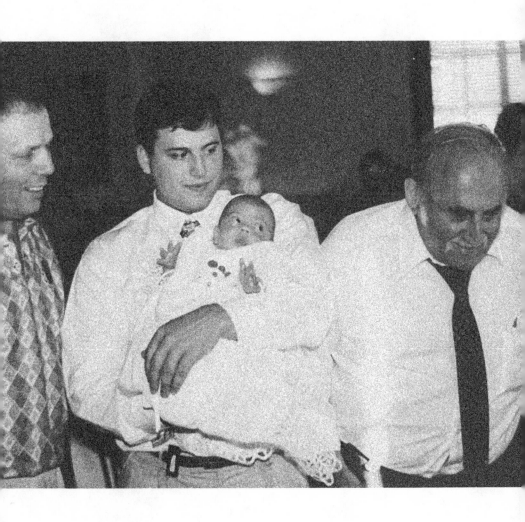

**Four generations
of Arillottas**

she would pray for me. Who knows, maybe her prayers were eventually heard. After all, I'm living a good life as a free man. There was a point when I thought I'd be strapped to a table having poison injected into my veins. But I'm still here, you bastards. I'm still here.

THE END OF AN EMPIRE

CHAPTER 24

After I got locked up for the murders of Bruno and Westerman, the organized criminals who once ran the Greater Springfield area had become less than organized. The Genovese family in New York had become a fading shadow in the streets of the South End of Springfield.

Most Made guys were dead or in prison except for a few of the older wiseguys. Mario Fiore and Frankie Pugliano were still doing some sports betting, but they remained low-key. They were smart enough to understand what had happened to the once-thriving empire that controlled the underworld of our area, and they didn't want to become part of that statistic. Going to prison in your mid-seventies can be a death sentence, and it's not a comfortable way to spend your remaining days on this earth.

Small crews are still involved in racketeering and running drugs, but they aren't under the direction of New York, and they aren't Made guys. The Manzis might still have a small circle of people dealing drugs out of their restaurant and they may be involved in sports betting and loan sharking. Albert, "The Animal" Calvanese, might still be running his operation, and if he is, he's one of the few who has successfully evaded the authorities for years. Whispers on the streets had him as a Made guy and a capo running things for the Genovese family, but this is nothing more than rumors. Albert is a lone wolf and always has been. He has done

Left to right: *Frankie Pugliano, Anthony Delevo, Billy Brown, Jerry Maloni, and Sam Harbey*

business with many connected guys, but he was smart enough to know that getting in too deep could get him locked up for a long time or get him killed. He enjoys his freedom too much to end up like that. I always liked and respected Albert for how he went about his business. Even though I believe he would have made a solid member of La Cosa Nostra, I get why he never went in that direction. Looking back, I wish I had made that same decision.

Things have changed in Springfield's South End. Spanish-speaking people have now infiltrated the once predominantly Italian section. As they began moving in, many Italians moved to the suburbs, where the streets were safer for their families. Mount Carmel social club, where Al Bruno was killed, has now become a place where the Latin Kings gang have held meetings. In the old days, this never would have happened. Their colors would have been shoved up their asses, and they would have been buried.

Mike Cecchetelli was running the gang and controlling a significant part of the drug trade in the area. His Uncle Dave used to be part of my crew, and as stated in a previous chapter, we tried hiring the Latin Kings for hit on Manzi, but they backed out.

Eventually, New Haven mobster Eugene "Rooster" Onofrio became a Made guy with the Genovese family. Guys like Ralphie Santaniello, Frankie Depergola, Johnny Calabrese, Gerald Danielli, and Richie Valentini began taking orders from Onofrio out of his New Haven office. Rooster was a very visible guy who would often be seen hanging out on the corner of Wooster Street in New Haven with a group of connected Italian guys.

According to a wire transcript from mobster John Rubeo who became a federal informant, Onofrio had several Springfield guys that he liked. He had proposed to the New York bosses that Ralphie Santaniello become a Made guy, and word had it that Frankie Depergola was angry that he was pushed aside because he had more street cred than his friend Ralphie. The books in New York were closed and neither of them were able to undergo the gun-and-knife ceremony.

▼ ▼ ▼

Things were quiet in our area until someone came up with the idea that they should approach a former Springfield Police Officer, who now ran a successful business, and try to extort money from him. Craig Morel, who author Joe Bradley graduated with at the police academy in 1986, built CJ's Towing Company into a multi-million-dollar company Morel started his own business out of a small garage in the Hungry Hill section of Springfield. He had one tow truck and was barely making ends meet until he was approached by Bruno. Morel knew if he was able to get the city towing contract he would become a millionaire, and he made a deal with the devil.

He was awarded the contract in 2000 while Mike Albano was Mayor, and Albano was connected to Bruno—the mayor made it happen. The rumor was Albano was paid a hefty sum for arranging the city towing contract to go to CJ's Towing. This has never been substantiated.

Over time, Morel would build his business from one tow truck to over sixty and his dream came true. After Bruno was killed, Morel thought his deal died with the boss and he was free and clear. It wasn't going to be that easy.

Ten years after Bruno was killed, Depergola, Daniele, Santaniello, Calabrese, and Valentini decided to pay a visit to Morel and extort fifty thousand dollars in back tribute they said was now owed to them. Santaniello threatened to cut off his head and bury him in his backyard. So what did Morel do? Being a former cop, he went to the FBI, agreed to wear a wire, and began recording his interactions with the careless crew. Morel agreed to pay them twenty thousand dollars as a start, with monthly payments to follow. With federal money, Morel went to the meeting and paid them off. It should not have been a surprise when the FBI arrested the crew for extortion, but apparently it was. In 2016, the gang of extorters were arrested, convicted, and sent to prison.

▼ ▼ ▼

In 2014 the Rubeo wiretap of Onofrio, the feds had him bragging that he was the boss of the Springfield Crew and that he was going to make some significant moves. After the arrest of the Springfield Crew for extortion, Onofrio later called them "a bunch of girls."

In July of 2018, in Manhattan Federal Court, Onofrio was sentenced to thirty months in prison for loan-sharking. He tried to get leniency by stating he was just a senior citizen trying to supplement his income by making high-interest loans and selling untaxed cigarettes—he was released early due to the Covid-19 pandemic.

The days of "Big Nose Sam" Cufari, Francesco "Skyball" Scibelli, "Big Al" Bruno, and Anthony "Bingy" Arillotta are over. It all came crashing down after a connected guy from the New York family began poking around Springfield. John Bologna was toxic to our thing in Springfield, and he turned out to be a federal informant. Had Bologna been whacked years before like he should have, the empire that once stood tall might still be thriving today. Instead, like the Roman Empire, it was reduced to rubble, and it's doubtful that it will ever be rebuilt. But while we reigned, it was glorious. We were on top of the world.

MY NEW
LIFE

EPILOGUE

I walked out the door, took a few steps, and looked back at the place I had called home for the last seven years. I thought about the many bad guys I lived with, the many corrections officers who had controlled my life, and the regimented daily routines I endured. I thought about the many friends I had made and some of the few good times we had while being locked up. I remembered the extreme violence that occurred inside and the lack of control I had over my life.

I survived and was now free, which felt good; but it came with a deep feeling of uneasiness. I had nothing but clothes on my back and a few bucks in my pocket. I was a convicted felon with a reputation as a murderer. Who would want to give me a second chance? Who would offer me a job? How would I be received by the world and the people back home? While incarcerated, I knew I had three hot meals daily and no responsibilities. All I had to do was try and stay out of trouble and stay alive—that seemed easy.

Now, I was looking at facing one of the most challenging times in my life. This time, I wasn't coming home as a Made guy with the biggest organized crime family in the country. I wasn't coming home to a pile of cash and rackets ready for me to take control of. There would be no big coming-home party thrown by goodfellas with high-end booze and Cuban cigars waiting to be consumed. I was starting fresh, and it was a little scary. I had never been a regular citizen with a regular job. As far back as I can remember, I was a gangster—that's all I knew. The unknown was deeply distressing.

My friends Louie Santos and Tony Rico came to pick me up. Seeing them waiting for me was a good feeling, and I appreciated them taking the long five-hour drive to New Jersey to greet me as a free man.

The drive home was filled with questions about my time inside, and we talked about what had been happening in the neighborhood over the past several years. I had been away for a long time. To put it into perspective, when I went away, Obama was at the beginning of his first term, and when I got out, Trump was in office. After arriving at my mother's house, we had a nice dinner, and I went to bed early. I was used to going to bed around nine-thirty, so my internal clock was shutting down.

I was no longer behind bars, but I wasn't completely free. I was on probation for three years and had to follow the rules. My probation officer would come by the house once a month to check up on me—see how the job search was going and how I was doing overall. I had to keep my nose clean, or else I could quickly end up right back in the joint. But a tiger can't completely change its stripes. I am Anthony Arillotta, and I used to rule the Springfield underworld. I was back, still alive and kicking, and I wouldn't be isolated.

The first place I went to was the Italian club. I stayed for a couple of drinks, playing it cool by sitting in the corner and sipping a nice glass of scotch. I was greeted by some of the local guys who seemed happy to see me and welcome me home. Others just looked my way and turned their backs. I knew some people would look at me with disdain, but they didn't know what I went through and what my options had been when I cooperated. Would they have chosen the needle or life without parole? Or would they have done what I did and made a preemptive strike? I think most would have made the same decision I did.

Someone had told me that I should be careful and watch my back. It wasn't meant as a threat; it was out of concern, and I gave that some thought. Should I carry a gun with me when I leave the house? What if I got caught with it? I'd end up in cuffs again. I couldn't risk that. I knew there was always a chance that someone would come collecting their revenge, and I could take a couple to the back of the head. After all, I was involved in killing the boss. Some people in the community liked Bruno, and he had family members who probably fantasized regularly about killing me. And then there was always the guy who wanted bragging rights. "I killed the guy who killed the boss." What was I to do? After all, I did spend most of my adult life knowing I could be clipped at any time. When you're a player in the big game like I was, you never know when the grim reaper will come calling. It was just a fact of life in La Costa Nostra. I was resigned to not spend my days worrying about it. I was going to try and have a good time and enjoy my life—no matter if it was just a few days or a few decades.

As I sat in the Mardi Gras strip club bar, I watched as Victor Bruno walked in. He glanced at me and kept walking by, as I sat enjoying a drink and cigar. I would say he wasn't having any good thoughts about me at that point—I'm the guy who was found guilty in the murder of his father. We never spoke.

▼ ▼ ▼

I finally got a job in Enfield, Connecticut selling Nissans, but that job only lasted two days. The manager called me into his office and told me he had to let me go. Victor Bruno called and told him who I was and that I was responsible for his father's death. Victor asked my manager how he could employ a killer to work at his dealership? He threatened to go to the press and expose the dealership if he didn't fire me. I was let go immediately. I wasn't surprised that Victor did that, but I was pretty pissed off.

It took a while, but I landed another job selling cars. With all the negative press circulating around me, I couldn't even get a job at McDonald's in the Springfield area. I had to take a job seventy miles away in Norwich, Connecticut, at another Nissan dealership. The general manager knew who I was but was kind enough to give me a shot. I worked my ass off to be successful and I put in around fifty hours a week. Keep in mind, I had two and a half hours of commuting daily.

I had never understood what it was like to work a regular job, and I gained respect for the regular guy who punched a clock every day to survive. It was a grind, to say the least.

Selling cars came easy for me and I was able to catch on quickly because in my former life I was always selling something on the street. I was a top earner, and that didn't change just because I was now working at a legitimate job. Within three months, I was rated as the top salesman in the dealership. I was selling cars like it was lemonade in the desert. Things were beginning to turn around. I was making money, dating a few hot girls, and enjoying the good life again. I wasn't drinking Louie the Thirteenth Cognac, but I was doing alright. I enjoyed eating out at nice restaurants and smoking a nice cigar afterward. Occasionally, I would venture off to a casino with a friend and try my luck at the sports book or a table. I figured it was the closest I would get to the action at this point in my life.

Things were going well for me, and as luck would have it, I thought it would all be crumbling down on me again. Whitey Bulger was brutally murdered after being transferred to the same prison as Freddy Geas, and Freddy has recently been charged with Bulger's murder. Back in 2018, Freddy was a prime suspect, and it was all over the news, and when they showed Freddy's face on the television, they showed my face too because he was my right-hand man. I was walking past a couple TVs outside the car showroom where customers sat waiting for their cars to be repaired, and my face was all over the television. At that point I figured everyone would find out who I was and what I had done. Then I'd be in the hot seat again, waiting for my final paycheck—Freddy's final gift to me.

I was on the floor when the sales manager said, "Anthony, whack that bug." I looked at the bug on the floor and then back over to him, knowing he had found out who I was. He went into the general manager's office, and they were talking for quite a while. Through the window, they would glance at me every now and then—I knew I was the subject of conversation. I was thinking, should I just pack up my shit now and say goodbye? Later, the general manager told me all the managers knew about my past, but they were alright with it and wouldn't say anything to the corporate big dogs. I was somewhat relieved that my job was secure, at least for now.

I'm still here.
At Our Lady of
Mount Carmel club.

The day after I was released from prison, I began getting calls and letters from media outlets who wanted me to tell my story. Stephanie Barry, a local crime reporter contacted me asking if I'd be interested in having her write a book about my life. I wasn't ready at that time to tell my entire story, so I declined. Many other newspapers from Massachusetts and Connecticut reached out, but I wasn't interested. But I agreed to an article with *GQ* magazine, and they published a nice story about me—full page. I also did stories with *Forbes* magazine and *USA Today*. I knew I wanted to write a book about my life, but it had to be the right author and the right deal.

I had successfully sold cars for a couple of years, and the pandemic began spreading. Most of our sales team was let go, and I was one of them. Jobs were now going to be tough to find, and considering my infamous past, it would be harder for me to land on my feet.

I began to dabble in real estate buying and flipping houses and that kept me busy for a while and I made some money. I decided to start getting my story out there, but I needed to be reasonably compensated for it. I began doing podcasts and other interviews that would pay a decent price. I met a lot of former gangsters who were doing the same, and they gave me some good advice on promoting myself and furthering my career as a former wiseguy. I was part of a group of five mobsters on the *John and Gene* show, and we got five thousand views. I was featured on VladTV and told some of my story as a mobster on that show. Later, I had a podcast produced titled *Money, Mayhem, and the Mafia,* and that did well. *Fox Nation* was negotiating a deal with my agent, and we ended up doing a lucrative show titled *Mob Mentality.* I also did a big podcast with Elie Honig the former NY federal prosecutor who ran the Bruno murder case called *Up Against The Mob.*

At that point, I decided I should hold off on doing many more shows and wait until after our book came out and then I would do shows to promote the book.

The book writing idea came about after I had a conversation with a friend Diane about my desire to have a book written. I wanted to have my life story published and I asked her if she knew any authors. Diane said she knew a writer, and she called Joe, who'd written several crime novels, and he agreed to a three-way conversation. After meeting with Joe in person on several occasions, he agreed to take on the project under two conditions. The first was that he wanted to write the book in the first person—in my words. We would need to meet for many hours while I told my story, and the recorder was rolling. The second was that Joe wanted to not only tell my story, but also the history of the Mafia in the Springfield area dating back to prohibition. The story of how the Genovese family migrated north from New York to Springfield and all the murders and violence that took place back then through the present day. I agreed and said I wanted the book to be about our area, not just about me.

It would be the first book ever written about the many infamous gangsters in our area, and the murders, violence, money, corruption, and intrigue that goes along with that life. Here we are—the book has been written and published.

I also set up a meeting with me, Joe, and Brian Goodman. Brian, now a successful Hollywood director and actor, has shown interest in a possible movie deal based on the book.

▼ ▼ ▼

As for the Springfield Crew, whispers on the street are that Ralphie Santaniello has recently been straightened out by the Genovese family in New York, making him a newly Made guy in charge of the area. This can't be verified, however, because of the omertá code.

Over the past several years, Albert "The Animal" Calvanese has been running the Our Lady of Mount Carmel Club, which has been the headquarters of the Italian Mafia for decades. Albert is thought to have assumed control of the club by his own hand (not sanctioned) after the death and imprisonment of many of Springfield's wiseguys over a decade ago.

As friction between Albert and Ralphie and his father Amedeo—who are his cousin and uncle—increased, Albert had a police protective order put in place to prevent them from entering the club.

In March 2024, while Albert was recovering from a bad car accident in which he nearly died, Ralphie and Amedeo initiated a member vote to change the leadership of the club. After the members voted in their favor, the Santaniellos had the protective order lifted and they changed the locks at the club, assuming control.

It is believed that many members weren't happy that Albert allowed me back into the club after I got released from prison. Also, members didn't like the way the club was being operated, which included allowing the leaders of the Latin Kings gang to hold weekly meetings inside the club.

Is this a resurgence of the Mafia in Springfield, and how will Albert Calvanese react to the recent coup at the hands of his relatives, the Santaniellos? This remains to be seen.

ACKNOWLEDGMENTS

Anthony: Thanks to my father, an honorable, hard-working, and honest man who was a hero to me. Thanks too to my best friend "Pazzo," whose love and support after my arrest is the reason I'm a free man today.

Joe: I would like to thank our literary agent Matthew Valentinas for his efforts in finding a publisher for this book. Diane Scibelli Wytrych for connecting me and Anthony. Greg Huff for his valuable input on the manuscript. And finally, a huge thanks to Yvonne for all her love and support.

Joe Bradley is a former Springfield Police Officer with a master's degree in criminal justice. He lives in Connecticut with his wife and three children.

South End Syndicate is set in 10-point Sabon, which was designed by the German-born typographer and designer Jan Tschichold (1902–1974) in the period 1964–1967. It was released jointly by the Linotype, Monotype, and Stempel type foundries in 1967. Copyeditor for this project was Boutros Salah. The book was designed by Brad Norr Design, Minneapolis, Minnesota, and typeset by Westchester Publishing Services. Printed and manufactured by Lightning Source on acid-free paper.

Printed in the USA
CPSIA information can be obtained
at www.ICGtesting.com
JSHW021520290824
68880JS00001B/1